Walking in Love's Footsteps

Gary D. Hendricks

NEWMAN SPRINGS PUBLISHING
320 Broad Street
Red Bank, NJ 07701

First originally published by Newman Springs Publishing 2024

ISBN 979-8-89061-173-4 (Paperback)
ISBN 979-8-89061-174-1 (Digital)

Printed in the United States of America

To Tami, the love of my life

Introduction

Before you is a heartfelt story of the life of a young girl that was severely raped and abused. Having survived, she would be forever blessed with a good life. Tested, tempted, knocked down, and failing, she got up every time and never gave up on the love she had for others and those who deeply loved her.

Society as a whole often ponders,

(1) Why is a drug addict haunted by drugs yet still uses them?
(2) Why does a gambler imperil his family financially even though he dearly loves them, still gambling?
(3) Why do alcoholics still drink even though the liquid, in reality, is sucking the spirit out of them?
(4) Even though women who have been molested and raped put the predator and their ghost behind them, why do some still risk not only their lives but also their relationships with their spouse, their significant other, or their family?

The ghosts of any addiction, thought long ago put to rest, is still restless, patient, waiting and hoping for the day of their resurrection.

Tami's touching story reveals her challenges, setbacks, and tremendous accomplishments.

The first chapter is very graphic, depicting a tragedy that forever changed Tami. The rest of her story is of her survival and the triumphs of her ensuing life.

From being a victim to being blessed with an incredible journey through life, she offers love and hope to young women and women who suffer as victims. Tami also offers a hopeful prayer in warning parents that predators can be anybody as they patiently wait for an opportunity.

1

Born eight years after her third sister, Tami often referred to herself as the "uh-oh" baby. With both parents working to put the older daughters through college and handle wedding expenses, she was raised in a different family environment. With parental time now a precious commodity, instead of one-on-one parenting, she mostly looked after herself. Showered with gifts and special Friday-night dinners, love encapsulated in her allotted time, Tami flourished.

The underestimation of Tami and her short stature started at a very early age. Starting in kindergarten, she waited patiently in front of her house for the school bus. Approaching, the school bus driver waved as he roared past her. Confused and rattled yet undaunted, she eventually made it to school.

Tami was nervous as the teacher asked the new students, "Who knows their whole name?" Full of confidence, she quickly raised her hand. Repeating what she heard her mother, Imara, say many times when trying to get one of her four daughters to answer, she would shout out the first and rhyming middle names, starting with the oldest daughter and ending it with "Dammit, Tami Faye, answer me!"

With that so eloquently repeated, Tami's next stop was to the principal's office, where she waited for her father, Bob. Returning home, undaunted and spirit unbroken but forever outspoken, she was a fighter and seldom in her life used any filters. At an early age, when asked what she wanted to be when she grew up, Tami—smiling, confident, and consistent—always answered, "A mommy!"

Sitting in the front row, watching her family unit consist of five women and one man, she saw time and time again Bob positioning himself as the affable good cop. He consistently set up Imara, the taskmaster, to be the bad cop. She remembered on one occasion a verbal disagreement that arose between one of her teenage sisters and Imara escalating. Bob's solution consisted of gathering the remaining noncombative family unit and declaring, "We're going for a drive while you two work this out."

Later in life, Tami, once making her father so upset with her, he demanded, "Go get me something to spank you with." Using her ingenuity, she returned with a handful of toilet paper. Laughing, Bob rewarded her for fast thinking and commuted her punishment.

As she progressed through grade levels, Tami was blessed with many friends; and soon, with all the sisters gone, she looked at her newfound freedom from having three less mothers to answer to. As they all lived in a very small community, the oldest sister once witnessed her driving her parents' car and several friends around town.

Happy and popular at school, Tami came home alone every day until her parents returned from work. As Tami was very good with young children, her afternoon job consisted of babysitting the neighbor's kids. Doing what she loved and being paid for it was too good to be true.

A nurturing, kind, and trusting child, she would read to the children and also played games with them until their father returned home from work.

At the tender age of thirteen and a half, Tami was already blessed with a full figure. A biological curse, yes, but the most grievous consequence was not possessing at this young age the mental skills to manage or even be aware of the temptation her innocent body attracted.

The only clue she had about sex was not from her mom but from living in a farming community. There, it was pretty easy to skip the "the birds and the bees" discussion. All a self-aware teenager had to do was observe the horses in the springtime gallivanting around and mating. Putting it all together as it unfolded each year answered any and all sexual questions.

In nature, predatory animals carefully observe their prey while sizing them up. Hunting and stalking, they control the when and the where. The biggest deception a predator plays is using a mask that camouflages their desire and intent.

Coming home, the kids' father greeted his kids and Tami as she stayed until she was paid and relieved from her babysitting duties. After excusing himself and going upstairs, he would always take a quick shower. Coming down the stairs, the predator was always masked in a bathrobe.

At first nudging and then putting his arm around Tami, he slowly adjusted the degree of physical contact as his kids played in front of them.

The predator, godless and full of lust and confidence, unseen by his kids, would hug Tami while pulling up the back of her shirt. He would rub her naked back with his naked pelvis as he tightly held her.

The *sexual abuse* intensified each time until Tami was now isolated and controlled in the bedroom, naked, terrified, helpless, hopeless, confused, alone, and worst of all, *silenced*.

Daily she was subjected to the worst sexual abuse and rape that lasted for many months.

He would choke Tami until she lost consciousness, and many times she had no idea what happened to her.

The predator, advancing, acted out his possessed evil, inflicting horrific pain and suffering as he performed his exorcism on Tami's psyche, causing permanent damage to her mind, body, and soul. She would carry those scars for the *rest of her life*.

Outside in the still, cold darkness of the night, Tami, despondent, silently prayed her last prayer, as her final rape was the most horrifying of them all.

He took Tami out to his wooded shed close to her house. Calling this human an animal or predator would be an insult to them. As a final act, the demon violated Tami with his rifle. When finished, to make a terrifying point, he fired the unheard bullet into the side of the shed.

Part of a victim's fear of a predator consists not only what they have done but also, worse yet, what they can still do, predicated on the *known* life-changing damage caused by the *rapes* and the fear and terror of the yet *unknown*. After every *rape*, the demon would say to Tami, "You tell anyone, and I will kill you and your family."

As her husband, the horror she went through was revealed to me over the twenty-seven years of marriage. Like a five-thousand-piece puzzle, each piece was painfully revealed to me one piece at a time. When the puzzle was finished, 444 unseen pieces still remained closely guarded and hidden in the box.

Tami revealed to me one of the mystery pieces many years into our marriage. Tami would never let me snuggle naked while holding her from behind.

Sharing this one puzzle piece with me, I understandably understood that the victims of sexual abuse and rape live with the horrors and collateral damage inflicted on them and can never dig a grave deep enough to cover the pain.

The one thing the demon tried but could not break was the forever spiritual love Tami had for her Savior, Jesus Christ.

❧ **2** ☙

Lying in bed, lost, Tami stared at the lifeless ceiling. Her mind overwhelmed, she desperately tried to find a way out of her tortured life while salvaging any remnants of hope.

She heard her parents' muffled words from their bedroom growing louder. Imara tapped on her door.

Slowly opening it, Imara stepped in with her father in tow.

Imara, upbeat and cheerful, said, "Tami! Dad and I are going to run some errands. Do you need anything?"

In a soft voice, she answered, "No, Mom. I am fine."

Imara walked past her dad as he stood and stared at her for a moment. "Love you, tiger," he said as he turned and shut the door.

Staring at the door, she whispered to herself, "Mom, Dad, I love you too."

After waiting for an affirmation that never came, Tami gathered all her courage and slothfully arose to get dressed. Going into the bathroom, she avoided the mirror. At this point in her life, she hated looking at the image of what she had become. She reached into the drawer and pulled out a double-edged razor blade. She wrapped one side of the razor with toilet paper. She turned and walked through the house. Opening the front door, she slowly proceeded out to the back yard.

For no rhyme or reason, Tami stopped to look at her mother's tulips. Taking a nervous shallow breath, she gazed at the wonderful Easter colors as this was her last vestige of peaceful beauty on Earth. Suddenly one of the tulips popped opened, innocently reveling its untouched inner beauty. She took this as a sign from God sending her a silent message: "Tami, there are reasons yet unknown for you to live. Your life is not done yet."

Frozen for a moment, focused on the tulip, she nodded her head in understanding. Peacefully she felt the weight of hopelessness leave her body and the power of her long-surrendered courage return. Taking the razor blade, she walked over to the garbage. After throwing the abandoned instrument away, she went back into the house.

Waiting patiently in the living room, Tami greeted her parents as they came in.

Standing firm, she forcefully announced, "I don't want to babysit anymore. No, let me change that. I won't babysit anymore."

Imara exchanged bewildered looks between her and Bob. Concerned, she asked, "Why not? Those kids love you, and they would be devastated at not having you as their babysitter—"

Cutting her mom off, she sternly determined, "Mom, I need both of you to go over and tell June I am sorry, but I want to concentrate on school. That is what I want. That is what I need."

Imara nodded her head in understanding. "Well, Bob, let's go and get this over with."

From the living room window, she watched her parents walk over to the neighbor's house until they disappeared from view.

She was terrified and frozen with fear. Her heart pounded as she prayed and questioned herself, "By me taking this action, is he going to think I told my parents and carry out the threat I heard so many times?"

Minutes seemed like hours. Suddenly she saw her parents walking back to the house. She took a deep breath. She felt as if the whole world had been lifted off her shoulders.

Walking in, her mother, in a matter-of-fact tone, said, "Well, it is done. June says thank you for all you have done and the children will miss you. She also said you are welcome to come over and see them anytime you want!"

Tami, grateful, jumped to her feet and hugged her parents. "Thanks, Mom and Dad. I love you."

Years later, when Tami was in her early twenties, she ran into June. After they exchanged pleasantries, June soon asked, "As you know, I divorced my husband long ago, but I have always worried that he might have molested you… Did he?"

With eyes widened, Tami took a deep breath before saying, "June, I am sure you know by now your husband was a possessed monster. No, he did not molest me…much. He went way beyond that. He tortured both my body and my brain by the rapes he executed. I have long ago tried to forget, but they were so horrific that some days, I am still numb to reality." As tears flowed down June's cheeks, Tami continued, "The past is the past, but some pasts are reignited by an event or situation that triggers an emotional reaction or decision. The sad reality is *this* really happened to *me*. Because of what was done to me, I will live with this the rest of my life, suffering from the emotional damage caused by the rapes."

June, in a whimpering, choked voice, said, "I am so sorry. I have failed you and others. I also will live with this the rest of my life. Please forgive me."

Knowing different, Tami stepped forward, put her arms around June, and lovingly hugged her. She then whispered, "June, we are all victims. I don't blame you, and there is no need for me to forgive you. You yourself were trying to survive, and what happened was not your fault. The fact that you didn't know *saved* your life. Did he steal my childhood? Yes. But did I let him steal the rest of my life? *No*, even though it still causes me trouble in my life from time to time."

*****

Starting ninth grade rejuvenated, Tami was excited to be back in school. She soon struck up a friendship with a young redheaded cowboy named Travis. Despite already going steady with another girl, within the next two months of the school year, Travis and his girlfriend broke up. Devastated, Travis turned to Tami's friendship, and soon they began building a relationship.

Travis himself had his trials. With both parents divorcing, he bounced from one house to another, living with his dad on some days and his mother on others. When he stayed with his dad, who was unfettered in his comings and goings, he had free, unmonitored access to the liquor cabinet. The downside in living with his mom was that she charged Travis for room and board!

Anxious to send a signal and permanently close and lock the door from the rapist, Tami invited Travis over to meet her parents.

Travis was just a few months younger than Tami and lived in a farming community, so Travis driving his dad's old truck without a driver's license was no big deal.

Tami, on seeing Travis pull up, thought the timing could not have worked out better. She hugged Travis as he got out of the truck. They then held hands as they walked across the front yard. Peeking out from the corner of her eye, she carefully watched the predator's reaction, which was forever frozen in her mind. She likened his look to a famished wolf dejected after chasing a young female elk and eventually giving up.

Sadly, though, she knew a predator's hunger is never satiated, and he could never be satisfied.

As she dealt with her past, Travis not only provided her protection but also comfort.

Attending seminary, he would always pour his beer into an empty soft-drink can to share with Tami. Also, with Travis having wheels, heavy petting took place always, and it was just short of going too far.

Travis helped Tami start her healing process. As she shared some of the horrific events she had endured, he listened with compassion and love.

Together they helped each other cope and navigate what life had dealt them and the yet undealt cards in their deck. They were still too young to understand that first love seldom lasts but always leaves a lasting impression…forever.

— ❧ 3 ❧ —

As time passed, Tami's life was about to change forever. With her sister about to get married, the family found out their pending son-in-law's brother, Dirk, could fix televisions. Soon after they invited him over, he busily started to disassemble the TV's inner workings. Tami, on seeing him, took an instant liking to him. He was quiet, kind, very shy, and best of all, easy on the eyes. Now almost fifteen and a half, Tami had grown into a full-figured young woman, outspoken and confident.

She walked over to the TV, leaned over the top, and, in a very soft voice, asked, "You sure you know what you're doing? Because if you don't, after my sister marries your brother, this is going to be my only form of entertainment!"

As Dirk looked up, the first thing to catch his eyes was her long cleavage, which, ironically, brought confirmation of the old seventy's slang referencing the TV as a boob tube!

Dirk, stammering but confident in his ability, answered, "Yes… it just needs a few tubes replaced."

Thrusting her hand down, she said, "Hi, I'm Tami!"

As they shook hands, Dirk firmly spoke, "Hi, I am Dirk. I guess when your sister and my brother get married, we will be sort of related."

Giggling, Tami teased, "Does your brother know what he is getting himself into?"

Dirk, smiling, retorted, "I could ask the same question concerning your sister!"

Soon after the wedding, Tami and Dirk started dating. Much to Tami's parents' dilemma, many issues arose, especially the eight-year difference in age, with Dirk being twenty-three.

In the fall of 1977, Tami started her sophomore year in high school. Wanting to have Travis in at least one of her classes, she made sure she did everything possible to have the same math class. Throughout Tami's life, she thrived by being able to maintain friends and relationships, both at the same time. While dating Dirk, she also remained good friends with Travis.

They were polar opposites. Dirk, as a teenager, was enthralled by electronic kits. His idea of a perfect date was spending Saturday evenings at the now-defunct company RadioShack. A good son and brother to his family, Dirk served with honor on his LDS mission in Mexico. Nothing could ever test or shake his religious beliefs or his testimony.

Tami, forever holding a tender spot in her heart for Travis rescuing her, still found Travis funny, a little rebellious, and always adventurous.

As she got to know Dirk, she found he was the complete opposite from Travis, which made him mysteriously all the more magnetic. Dirk was a man of few words, but Tami more than made up any lack of conversation. Going to the movies, dinner, and outdoor adventures, they quickly got to know each other and, subsequently, each other's parents. It wasn't long before Dirk and Tami's father struck up a deep friendship. With plenty of things to fix, Bob kept Dirk busy.

At Dirk's house, Dirk's father was the salt of the earth. He was pure, simple, hardworking, and a part-time farmer. Most of all, he was proud to have deep pioneer roots seeded in the LDS Mormon faith. Dirk's mom was kind and soft-spoken, not to mention a stalwart homemaker that possessed an infectious giggle that brought a smile to your face.

Dirk was a stranger to dating. His only girlfriend experience was named Pearl. Tami, who sometimes harbored jealousy, penned a song she would sing to Dirk: "Pearl! Pearl! Pearl! You're as ugly as a squirrel."

As time passed and they got to know each other more emotionally, one afternoon, Dirk and Tami were upstairs in his bedroom with the door closed. As they lay clothed together, events soon turned heavy. Suddenly bolting up, mad at both himself and Tami, Dirk scolded, "What are you doing to me?"

Defending herself in anger, Tami retorted, "Hey! This is what Eve should have told Adam! 'We *both* took a nibble from the apple, and it *takes* two'! I can wait, and I will wait. But I have feelings, and one of the strongest feelings I have now is not anger…but love."

Humbled Dirk said, "Tami, I am sorry. You are right, and yes, I love you."

After that day, both Dirk and Tami settled down as their love continued to grow stronger each passing day.

She still hung around with Travis at school. He always made Tami feel adventurous. There were some alone times together as their feelings of a deeper and more fulfilling friendship was always there. One such instance was where, on a whim, they decided to ditch class and ended up in the adjoining park next to the high school. They made out at the top of an old playground's tubular climbing structure in the shape of a rocket ship.

Opinions matter to some, and excuses abound. Tami, unsettled, being deeply affected by her past, greatly exposed and exasperated many of her decisions when it came to physical feelings toward teenage boys and men.

*****

At Dirk and Tami's first Christmas Eve together, they drove to the mall. Excited but unsure, Tami remained nervous and in suspense as to what Dirk was going to get her for Christmas and where he was taking her.

They walked around the packed mall full of last-minute shoppers. As they passed a store, Dirk suddenly pulled Tami back and into a jewelry store.

He gave Tami a quick reassuring glance. "I thought we would look at some rings."

She held his hand, scared, as she silently followed.

They approached a smartly dressed salesman who warmly spoke, "May I help you?"

Dirk never broached the subject of a marriage proposal with a question. Smiling back at Tami, Dirk cleverly and with surety said, "We would like to look at some engagement rings please."

Tami's heart was pounding. She remained silent. Together they followed the salesman.

Reaching into the display case, the salesman asked, "What cut of diamond were you two looking for?"

Nervous, Dirk turned his head and gazed at his still shocked and speechless girlfriend as he stood at the precipice of acceptance or rejection. Then he smiled. He immediately saw in Tami's eyes the answer he wanted to hear.

Stepping closer to the case, dazzled by the sparking diamonds, Tami confessed, "I don't know. Can I try some on to see which one we like?"

The salesman, pulling out a tray and laying it on the glass countertop, said, "An excellent idea!"

After spending some time at the store, they soon agreed on the cut of the diamond and the price, and lastly, they took Tami's ring size measurements. All this merriment happened on the Christmas Eve of 1977. Dirk and Tami were engaged.

With all the excitement of buying the engagement ring, the biggest trick had yet to be played: selling this act to each other's parents!

4

Taking the path of least resistance, Dirk and Tami decided to break the news to Dirk's parents first. Gathering his parents together, he escorted them into the living room as an unspoken aura of excitement and suspense permeated the room.

Sitting next to Tami on the couch, Dirk nervously cleared his throat as he softly began to speak, "Mom, Dad, I have appreciated your support and the love that you have shown Tami. Today I bought Tami an engagement ring as this is the woman I want to spend the rest of my life with."

Tami exchanged a quick glance with Dirk, then quickly focused her attention to Dirk's mom. She said, "Teresa, I want you to know how much I love your son, and we are asking for your blessing and support in letting us get married."

Teresa, sitting in a chair across from the kids, brought her closed fingers to her lips and pondered. Tilting her head down thinking, she stared at the well-worn rug. Focusing her eyes on Joseph, in a calm voice, she asked, "Joseph, what do you think?"

Joseph, calmly sitting in his chair, relaxed, beamed at the news. Upbeat, he spoke, "Son, I have long dreamed of the day that you would find someone as loving as Tami to share your life with. I think this is an excellent Christmas gift for the both of you—and us. You have my blessing!" Turning his head, he said, "Mom, what do you think?"

Teresa smiled as she nodded her head and said in a soft motherly voice, "I am so happy for you two, and yes, you also have my blessing too!"

All rose and exchanged loving hugs of acceptance and happiness. Their oldest child was getting married!

After waving goodbye, Dirk and Tami's next stop was Tami's house to break the news to her parents.

Along for the ride, anxiety and uncertainty accompanied them to their next destination…and destiny.

Tami led the way into the house and was relieved at seeing her parents alone and free from babysitting grandkids. As they sat at the dinner table, Tami and Dirk joined them.

Bob, putting down the newspaper, was happy to see them. "Well, hi!"

Imara, smiling, asked, "What have you two been up to this afternoon?"

Tami innocently responded, "Oh, we did some last-minute Christmas shopping!"

Bob, excited, asked, "What did you get us, or is it supposed to be a surprise?"

Tami jumped at the perfect opportunity. She interjected and said, "Oh, it is a surprise, and I hope you two will like it! Dirk bought me an engagement ring!"

Nothing could describe the shocked, speechless look on Imara's face as she silently gathered her thoughts off the floor. Bob, smiling, took the course of kicking his can just a little bit farther down the road and defaulted back to Imara as he waited for her comments.

Imara was not exactly happy with the eight-year age gap; and Tami, a still-developing youth, was just starting high school. Imara, harboring her carefully guarded opinion, thought Tami still had a lot of growing up to do and a life full of adventure ahead of her before finally settling down and getting married.

Imara, ready, calmly spoke, "Well, you two, this truly tops any Christmas surprise I have ever had. To be honest, I am very concerned about Tami being too young to get married. Are you two sure this is what you want?"

Dirk, giving Tami a quick reassuring glance, replied, "Yes, Mrs. Westley. I love Tami very much, and I know both of you have very mixed feelings about this. Please know and understand I will be a good husband and take good care of her. Mr. Westley, I will also be a good father and husband, just as you have been to your family."

Tami, in a gentle, loving voice, said, "Mom, Dad, you have been wonderful parents, and I know you have concerns. But I love Dirk, and I just know this was meant to be."

Rising from his chair, Bob reached out to shake his hand, "Congratulations, Dirk, and I am happy for both of you." Grinning with happiness, he commented, "My little tiger is getting married! I love you!"

Tami stood and hugged her father, holding back her tears of happiness. In an emotional voice, she responded, "I love you too, Dad. Thank you two for supporting and understanding us."

Both turned to Imara and hugged her as Dirk spoke first. "Imara, thank you, and I love you. I will forever love and cherish your daughter."

Tami lovingly expanded on Dirk's words: "Mom, I won't disappoint you and will follow your example as a wonderful wife and mother. I love you very much."

Finished, all four migrated into the living room and sat around the Christmas tree, visiting until it was time for Dirk to go home. They all rose to say goodbye. Dirk gave a quick kiss on Tami's cheek. He held her and gently hugged her.

Dirk and Tami walked out to Dirk's car. After hugging and kissing again for the longest time, Tami softly said, "Thank you for loving me and being in my life."

Dirk, smiling like he had never smiled before, said, "I am the luckiest man to have ever found you. I promise I will love you forever."

5

Going back to school after the Christmas break, Tami, excited, announced her engagement to all her friends; and their opinions, judgment, and gossip quickly spread.

Within a few weeks, the right opportunity presented itself as Tami and Travis decided to ditch school and go hang out at Travis's dad's house. They helped themselves to a few drinks from the complimentary unmonitored liquor cabinet; and before long, impaired judgment, bad decisions and uncontrollable hormones led to Tami and Travis surrendering their virginities.

The difference between good judgment and bad judgment is not thinking about the consequences. But there are always consequences.

That's the one thing about grace. You will be forgiven, but deep inside yourself, you can never get back what you lost.

On returning to school, Tami soon ran into one of her girlfriends. She shot a suspicious look and knew Tami ditched school with Travis. She abruptly voiced her disapproval, exclaiming, "You had sex!"

Busted, Tami knew she was in trouble, and before long, the summation of her engagement announcement to Dirk yet just having had sex with Travis would soon spread all over school. That was something she would not or could not face.

After returning home, Tami waited impatiently for her parents to return. She knew her sister Candice and brother-in-law Paul, now living in Mesa, would help her. The only thing left for her to do was quickly formulate a plan to sell to her parents.

As she and her parents were gathered at the dinner table, Tami put her fork down only after a few bites and broke the silence, saying, "Mom, Dad, I have been thinking. Maybe I am rushing into this too fast and need to take some time to make sure that my engagement to Dirk is truly the right decision. I want to go live with Candice and Paul and finish my sophomore year there so I can have some time to think."

Imara shocked, succeeded in keeping both her relief and joy of the news masked, asked, "Bob what do you think?"

Bob, glancing at Tami, smiled. "If Paul and Candice say it is okay, I don't have a problem with that. Besides, Candice can probably use your help with their newborn baby."

Imara jumped up, went to the phone, and quickly dialed their number. After a lengthy conversation, all were in agreement. Tami would fly out the next day while Candice contacted the school district to register her.

In no mood to eat and troubled, Tami got up and went to call Dirk. As she heard ring after ring, her heart pounded, and her mind raced, thinking about what she would say. After hearing Dirk's voice, Tami calmly said, "Hi, Dirk!"

Dirk, upbeat and excited, replied, "Hi, Tami! So glad you called as I have been thinking about you all day!"

Tami softly and gently said, "So have I. Hey, the reason I wanted to call you, and I know this is sudden, but I am going down to Mesa tomorrow for a while to help my sister with her newborn baby."

Dirk's voice gave away that he was saddened and disappointed. "How long are you going to be gone?"

Tami, also saddened by indirectly hurting Dirk, was more disappointed in herself by her repentant action. She was unsure of both the question and herself. "I don't know, and I am sorry. I know letters and phone calls will never make up for actually being together. But I have to do what I have to do."

Dirk, in a sweet, loving voice, said, "I understand. Just know I love you very much."

Tami was emotional, her voice cracking. "I love you very much too, and I am sorry that I have to leave you."

Tami hung up the phone, ashamed. Hidden tears flowed down her cheeks as she went to her room to start packing.

That night, as Imara and Bob lay in bed, Imara faced Bob, relieved, and confessed, "Well, maybe this will work out for the better. Tami is just too young to get married. I cannot bear to see her suffer the embarrassment and the gossiping behind our backs that I know will take place. It will be just like it was when the Beckers' sixteen-year-old daughter got married."

The next morning, Bob and Imara quietly drove Tami to the airport, each unsure of what to say and how to say it. They guarded their thoughts and emotions. Together, Bob and Imara silently walked her to the gate and gave her a loving hug. Imara kissed her daughter goodbye and advised, "Now, you help out Candice and Paul with the baby. And don't cause any trouble."

Frowning, Tami said, "*Mom…I won't!*"

Bob, having trouble saying goodbye to his baby, hugged her. "Do well in school, tiger. We love you and are going to miss you."

Stepping back and smiling, Tami said, "I love you too. Daddy!" Turning to Imara, Tami said, "I love you too, Mom."

Taking her first step, Tami slowly turned to the gate. Confused, upset, disappointed, and unsure of herself, she walked down the ramp not as a passenger but a runaway.

*****

Life for Tami in Arizona was good. She was meeting new friends and classmates. The transition between schools went very well. Also helping Candice and Paul, Tami assisted with the housework and babysitting, which enabled Paul and Candice the opportunity and luxury of having a date night.

*****

With Tami's disappearance, Travis's life was not going well as he did not know what happened to her. She would never know what Travis went through or how much grief he endured, caused by their actions. Of course, in the seventies, in the weighing of truth for both guilty parties, males were labeled as sexual icons and the females as loose sluts. The sense of responsibility and the scales of truth were unjustly weighted in favor of the males.

Travis eventually dropped out of school and took a sanitation job. As he was new to the job, it didn't take very long for him to become a victim of an industrial accident. Travis was dumping trash cans in the back of the truck when his coworker, not paying attention, activated the scooping blade on the back of the truck and severed parts of Travis's three fingers on one hand.

*****

Toward the end of Tami's sophomore year, a junior asked her out on a date to the upcoming final dance of the year. Unsure, Tami called Dirk to ask what he thought. In his kindness and understanding, knowing their age difference, he gave her permission to go to the dance, which she did. After passing her sophomore year and saying goodbye to her classmates, she was sad to leave her friends but happily returned to be with Dirk.

Dirk met Tami at her house, and as Tami saw Dirk for the first time, something clicked. She knew he was the one as they embraced and passionately kissed.

Whispering in his ear, she lovingly exclaimed, "This is where I belong. I am home safely in your arms! I will never leave you again. I love you with all of my heart, my soul, and my spirit."

As Dirk hugged her tight, tears ran down his cheeks. "I missed you so much. I prayed that you would not change your mind and that you'd return to me. I am the happiest and luckiest man on earth to have you as my wife."

After a few days had passed, they both agreed that July 28, 1978, would be their wedding date. Coincidently, this was also the same anniversary date as Tami's parents'.

Hearing the news of the wedding date, Dirk's parents were overjoyed with happiness.

Tami's parents and sisters were still trepidacious about the marriage. Scheduled to go overseas, her parents, in one final attempt, offered a not-so-subtle bribe, enticing her to put off the wedding so she could go to Europe with them.

Deeply in love, she politely declined the offer.

On July 28, 1978, Tami and Dirk were married in the Ogden Temple for time and all eternity.

6

On their wedding day, having time between the Temple Marriage and the reception, Dirk and Tami, impatient and anxious, went to their small rental space in the basement of an old house.

On their return to the reception, Imara became furious to learn that their marriage had already been consummated. I guess that somewhere in her mother's mind, there were rules. To the newlyweds, they freely let their love, passion, and desire dictate the timing. With the festivities over, they spent their first night together in a hotel room in Salt Lake. The following day, they went to the mountains and spent the rest of their honeymoon camping.

Returning to a new normal, Tami would soon go back to a new school, and Dirk returned to work that would soon turn into a life-long career.

Years later into our marriage, Tami confessed to me that she ran into Travis at a fair and confessed, "When I saw Travis, I knew I had made the right decision to marry Dirk."

Time passed, and a few more pieces of the puzzle fell into place. Tami did meet Travis at a fair, but in reality, "a fair" was "an affair"—a shocking and head-turning event, but that was just Tami.

Whenever unsure, hurt, second-guessing herself, or tempted, she would always test herself and her feelings.

Looking ahead, the answer she sought was having a loving long-lasting relationship and a good husband and father. The man she loved and married could give her all of this.

Now solidified in her love for Dirk, at the end of December 1978, Tami was pregnant!

Going back to school after the Christmas break, it wasn't too long before Tami was transferred to a school for mostly unwed mothers, Tami being the rare exception. The curriculum was the same as high school except that there were some added courses including infant care and homemaking, and the mothers brought their infants to school with them.

Long past her due date, one night, Tami ate a generous portion of a large pizza. Soon after, she started having labor pains. Arriving at the hospital, she had a long night of contractions and an occasional revisit with the pizza!

Tolerant to pain, she quietly endured each mounting contraction. When the time came, Dirk accompanied Tami to the delivery room. Before long, she gave birth to a beautiful girl. Tami, describing to others Dirk's reaction toward experiencing the birth of his daughter, said, "Dirk walked in as a wonderful, supportive husband and feeling so blessed, and he floated out as a proud father." Meeting up later in Tami's room, together they held their daughter and named her Catherine Marie.

Returning to school with a very early preschooler, Tami, blessed with an oversupply of breast milk, also nursed the infants that needed extra nourishment.

As was part of Tami's character, she persevered as some of the girls ended up quitting school. Determined and dedicated, she finished high school and graduated proudly with her original high school classmates.

Soon after graduating, Tami took care of Catherine and also helped babysit and raise the kids of one sisters to earn extra money to help support her family. Dirk, working, continued earning advancements in the sign industry.

Still true to his religion, one day, Dirk was working on a sign and was told the power was off. As he worked on the wires, one grounded out, causing a large explosion of sparks around his body. The closest Dirk came to cussing that day in front of the other workers was saying the word *damn*. The workers, both regaled and shocked, exclaimed, "Dirk said the word *damn!*"

With Catherine approaching two, Tami and Dirk always hoped they would have more children. Tami soon developed a vaginal bleeding discharge that only got worse as the weeks went on. During some bleeding episodes, her hematocrit blood levels dropped so dangerously low that she was given massive transfusions of blood. The hope of having more children turned into the hope that somehow, a miracle would happen. Instead, they were given the prognosis of her needing a complete hysterectomy to live.

Getting married and having a child so young at seventeen, if Tami had waited later in life to marry, she would have never been able to have children. Miracles do happen for reasons we sometimes question but do not understand.

Tami and Dirk moved from their basement rental into a mobile home. Finally a mommy, Tami was happy and felt blessed for both her daughter and also her husband. Still doing well in the sign industry, Dirk was now a journeyman, which meant he was now fully trained and making good money.

Growing tired of their living accommodations, Dirk and Tami decided to build their own house. Building their dream home took a while as they did the majority of the work themselves with their families' help. Finished, they happily moved in to their own home, which was close to Dirk's parents.

Tami and Dirk attended their new church, and it wasn't long before Tami had met everyone and settled into their religious life and the community. Attending church one Sunday, Tami saw one of her friends, Peggy.

Tami could see she was upset by something and asked, "Peggy what's wrong?"

Peggy, holding back her tears, whispered, "I saw something on the hallway billboard that really upset me."

Both walked over, and Peggy showed her the picture of a heavyset woman with the caption below her reading, "Does this look like a child of God?"

Heavyset herself, Tami was also offended and said in a reverent, soft, determined voice, "I'll take care of this."

In a "Christlike" manner, Tami met separately with several of the assigned leaders. With very little time lost, a decision was made to have the picture and captioned removed.

Tami was never the type of person to gloat or harbor ill will. She forgave and moved on with her life. She did this with ease because of the love she had for Jesus and the religion she was born into and loved.

Dirk, soft-spoken and reserved, supported and loved his wife in all her endeavors and works without reservation or regret.

In his whole career, Dirk had worked for a small sign company and was proud of all the opportunities that had been afforded to him. One morning, after Tami dropped off Dirk at work, she soon received a phone call from him. Nervous, he told her the company had just been sold and was purchased by one of the biggest sign companies in Utah. Excited, Tami knew this meant more opportunities for her husband to grow and make more money.

Way ahead in the future of sign development, Dirk had studied and was experienced in electronics; and as Tami predicted, Dirk was promoted to a newly formed department to help install and sell electronic message signs.

With the acquisition of the company, Dirk and I now worked for the same company.

I had never met Dirk, Tami, or Catherine at this time, and this was because I worked in Las Vegas. That would soon be remediated as I was scheduled to attend an electronic course taught by Dirk in Logan, Utah.

Meeting and watching Dirk teach, I concluded I didn't think I ever met a man my age who could ever possess even wear a pocket protector!

Soft-spoken, intelligent, logical, Dirk was a carbon copy of Spock in the original TV series *Star Trek*. Dirk also had a firm grip on teaching all the data and detail to troubleshoot and repair any electronic sign display.

Remarking to me one time, Tami shared a story of her husband's "Spockisms" and confessed, "One time, I needed the trash to be taken out. I asked Dirk if he wanted to take the trash out the front door or the back door. Dirk stopped and was in deep thought, setting up in his mind a 3D visual mock-up. You could see his brain running the data comparisons of both routes and computed that the front door was a few steps closer. The he exclaimed, 'I'll take it out the front door!'"

Tami was smiling and shaking her head in bemused wonderment and thought, *I wonder how he knew* that*!*

As Dirk taught our class, although Dirk had the knowledge, the hardened group from Nevada was a handful.

Later that night, I stayed behind as the Nevada group left to find a bar. Invited up to visit with Dirk and his boss, I was about to meet for the first time in my life…Tami.

Walking into the motel room, Tami was carrying a sheet cake. In tow were two teenage girls that were living with them as Tami help them sort out life.

Tami did not realize it, but as she walked up the stairs, Tami's boobs had left their impressions on the cake—and in my mind too! In cutting the cake to serve, Dirk's boss lovingly joked, "I'll just cut around the boobs!"

The next morning, someone in the Nevada group indirectly teased, "What time do we cut the cake?" As the group laughed, I could tell it hurt Dirk's feelings. I came away from the class learning a lot about electronics. But I also learned the difference between Utah's care and hospitality and our Nevada group's rudeness and cruelty.

$$\sim\!\!\diamond\; 7\; \diamond\!\!\sim$$

There comes a time in life where a defining moment changes or alters our course in life.

That moment came with a telephone call from the manager of the Las Vegas service department.

Picking up the ringing phone, Dirk said, "This is Dirk. How may I help you?"

In an upbeat voice, the caller responded, "Dirk, this is Richard Bullock, the service manager from Las Vegas. I hope I didn't catch you at a bad time. Do you have a minute?"

Dirk was a little bewildered. "No, not at all. How can I help you?"

Suddenly Richard's voice became more serious. "Dirk, I am going to get right to the point. I have heard so much about you and your electronic knowledge. Also, you are very talented and are a hard worker. Our sales department just sold what is going to be the biggest electronic display on the Las Vegas Strip, and unfortunately, our current technician…well… He's just not going to be able to handle it, and frankly, I am concerned. I believe you might have had the opportunity to meet him when he came up to attend your electronics class."

Dirk, never wanting to ever talk bad about anyone, remained positive and answered, "Yes, I remember him."

Richard continued, "Well, I am asking if you and your family would like to transfer to Las Vegas and work for me, and before you answer that, the pay in Vegas is substantially higher than it is in Utah. I am prepared to offer you journeyman pay and a vehicle you can use both for work and pleasure, and we'll pay for the gas."

Dirk was astounded and shocked. "I…am honored that you called and also your offer. But with all due respect, I want to talk it over with my wife."

Richard, understanding, said in a respectful, reassuring voice, "Dirk, I totally understand. Call me back in a few days with your decision. You are going to love working in the Las Vegas division."

Returning home for the evening, Dirk opened the front door. It was a well-played custom that on hearing his car, Tami would always meet him at the door with a loving kiss. Seeing his coy facial expression, Tami tilted her head and giggled as she spoke, "What's up with you?"

Dirk smiled and grabbed Tami's hand. "Come over here to the couch. I have something to tell you!"

Never seeing her husband act like this, she sat. Her face exhibited a mystified, puzzled look. Tami was always able to read Dirk, but this time, she found no clues.

Dirk cleared his throat. "I received a phone call today from the Las Vegas service manager. He offered me a job in the electronics department, and it is a little more than twice what I am making now. He also offered a new car with unlimited use and a company gas card." Dirk, uncertain of Tami's answer, nervously questioned, "What do you think?"

With her face filled with excitement, Tami shrieked and expounded, "WHAT DO I THINK? This offer is a no-brainer! There is only one thing I need to do."

After seven years of being married, sometimes Dirk was almost afraid to ask. Confused, bravely queried, "What?"

Tami screamed in exhilaration, "I'll go start packing!"

*****

The family drove from Utah. Seeing Las Vegas for the first time is always an exciting and a unique experience for anyone. Tami got her first glimpse. She rolled down the car window. Putting her knees on the seat, with her hands holding on to the door, she arched her back for a better view. Her head and top part of her body were hanging outside the car, and her face was filled with excitement. As she absorbed the warm evening summer breeze, her eyes gleamed as if she was looking through the eyes of a child. The lights of Las Vegas overwhelmed and dazzled Tami, both fueling and filling her imagination with the promise of a bright future ahead.

After quickly finding a house, the family moved in and began settling down and planting their roots in the community. Not more than a few months had passed when the doorbell rang. Opening it, Tami was greeted by a man serving an eviction notice. Confused, she asked, "We have been paying our rent. How can this be?"

The man was sincere but blunt. "Miss, I feel terrible for you. But the owners of the house haven't been paying their mortgage."

Handing the notice to Tami, the man, truly saddened, softly spoke, "I am so sorry."

Devastated at losing their deposit money but undaunted and determined, they moved again just in time for Catherine to start school.

They all adjusted and met new friends. Dirk was doing well at work as Catherine excelled in being one of the top students gradewise. Tami the consummate homemaker, working in making a house into a home.

Las Vegas was definitely an adjustment for the family. Everything was out in the open.

Dirk and Tami were invited by their new friends to attend one of the premier adult-orientated shows on the Strip. As they all settled in, excited to be in the moment, doing something different for the first time, the lights dimmed. Suddenly the orchestra started to play as the curtain rose, quickly revealing the shimmering female dancers. Taking immediate notice, Tami, shocked, shrieked over the music and blurted out to Dirk and indirectly the other patrons seated nearby, "THEY'RE TOPLESS!"

Before long, with the family settled, Tami started a job close to home at a plus-size women's dress shop. She loved her job, and it wasn't too long before she was promoted to manager.

With that title also came very long and unpredictable hours. On many Saturdays, with Dirk also working, Catherine would play driving her battery-powered car in the back of the clothing store, making the best of it but not happy about it.

As Tami progressed in her work, the company took notice, and she was included along with other top-performing managers to go to Tucson, Arizona, to attend a three-day meeting.

Tami felt honored as this was the first time in Tami's life that she had been recognized for not only being an outstanding mom but also as a manager.

Arriving back at the hotel early, she took advantage of the alone time and decided to get a break from a stressful day of meetings. So she went down to the pool for a swim.

The only one swimming, she soon noticed that for some time, a man was standing on his second-floor balcony and intently watching her form.

Flipping on her back, Tami dove underwater and pulled down the top of her one-piece bathing suit. Resurfacing, Tami's breasts were now exposed as she floated on her back.

As the story was told to me many years later, Tami said that after she exposed herself, she rode up in the elevator with the man and, later on in the evening, ordered room service for dinner as she was afraid to venture out.

My question to Tami that I never got or ever wanted to ask was "If you rode up in the elevator with this man, to me, this meant he had to come down poolside to flirt with you, with you two leaving together. Well?"

Upon returning home, Tami soon began putting on weight and became the heaviest she had ever been in her life. To protect herself from herself and men, part of Tami's solution, she once confessed to me, was "I put on weight so no man would want me." In reality, the flip side of that coin was "I also put on weight so I would feel undesirable enough not to want other men."

Soon after that, Tami quit her job and became a stay-at-home mom, to the delight of both Dirk and Catherine.

*****

One afternoon, Tami received a call from Steve, an old high school friend.

They went back many years, and she was the first person he confessed to about being gay. They stayed in touch from time to time. He was very talented in the field of home decor, and he left to fulfill his passion in San Francisco, telling Tami, "I am going to rock San Francisco like nobody else has!"

Over the phone, Steve informed her he was back to living with his mom and his brother, Dave, had contracted AIDS, and was not expected to live long.

Steve was asking for her help, and she said she would come up within the next few days.

With Dirk home and Tami fixing dinner, she thought the best way to tell Dirk was at the dinner table.

As all were seated, Dirk led the prayer and blessed the food. Passing the food, Tami spoke first. "Dirk, you remember Steve, don't you?"

Nodding his head, Dirk replied, "Yes, I remember him. You went to school with him, and he moved up to San Francisco."

Tami continued, "Yes. I got a call from him today, and he is not doing well. As a matter of fact, he is dying."

Dirk's voice revealed he was stressed and concerned. "Oh no. What from?"

Bowing her head, she softly confessed, "AIDS." After pausing for a few minutes to let the moment sink in, she continued, "Dirk, he also called me because he needs my help. I would like to go up and take care of him for a few weeks, if that is all right?"

Dirk took a deep breath and, in a sympathetic tone, spoke, "Tami, I am worried about you doing this. This disease… They are still researching AIDS, and they don't know much about it other than it is highly contagious and deadly."

Wearing a worried look, Tami answered, "I know. But I also know that somehow, I will be protected. This is about helping out a fellow human being. Dirk, I will be careful."

With a loving smile, Dirk responded, "I know you will, and yes, you need to go. Just remember, you have two people here that deeply love you and need you too."

After leaving that morning, Tami attended to Steve's needs and wants. It was both hard work and constantly stressful, staying safe from the unknown yet providing the love and care needed.

In the end, as his internal organs failed, Tami and Dave were taking Steve to the hospital. Steve was lying down in the back seat, lifting his head up. On seeing a 7-Eleven sign, he shouted out the best he could, "SLURPEE!"

Quickly reacting, Dave turned the car around. As they came to a sudden stop, Tami bolted out of the car and ran in. Returning, she held the straw to Steve's dry lips. Unconscious, he was never able to drink it and passed away the next day.

A few days after she returned home, both Tami and I got to indirectly witness Steve rocking San Francisco on October 17, 1989.

I was with a friend at a Las Vegas bar, getting ready to watch game 3 between the Giants and Athletics. The only thing I knew was that the game was going to have to be postponed because of an earthquake. Tami, who was at home and watching the news, smiled to herself and said, "Well, Steve, you finally got to rock San Francisco!"

$$\sim\!\!\infty\, 8 \,\infty\!\!\sim$$

When I met Dirk and Tami in Logan, my wife and I were happily married for five years and the proud parents of two wonderful boys. My world as I thought I knew it was shattered on February 14, 1982.

The kids were in bed, peacefully sleeping; and Nancy and I were sitting in the living room, talking. Nancy was troubled. I could tell she hadn't been herself for the past two weeks. Wanting to cheer her up, I cajoled, "Hey, Nancy, it's Valentine's Day. What can I do to cheer you up?"

Nancy was looking down. She slowly raised her head and said with a steady, nonemotional voice, "I feel so ashamed and disappointed in myself." She paused for a moment and avoided eye contact. Then she took a deep breath before she continued. "I need to confess something to you. I met someone years ago, just a few months before our first anniversary. This person either came in or called me at the bank with questions about his account and made small talk at least twice a day. Persistent, he flirted and pressed me every day to go out with him even though I told him I was married. Eventually, I went over to his condo one evening where I was supposed to be at my ceramics class, and we eventually had sex. That, in turn, developed into an affair that lasted about six months."

I was shocked, hurt, and devastated. My body quivered as my brain froze. Searching for words that never came, I tried to catch Nancy's eyes and body language, which yielded no clues.

Gathering my thoughts the best I could, I finally spoke, "Why are you telling me this now?"

Nancy, immediately answering, confessed, "I always thought it was because I was young. Meeting you when I was sixteen, I felt I missed out on something. After the affair was over, it was over. And then we had kids, and I was now a mother. This person's birthday was on the sixth of February, and I called him to wish him Happy Birthday. With the well-wishes over, he then begged me to come over to his house. I did, and things went too far. And we ended up in bed."

The only thing I could focus on or think about was that I was happily married to the love of my life and had two precious children. Now I was being told what I always perceived as real was now all a ruse. One thing I knew for certain was that I would stay with Nancy for the sake of the kids as I still loved her. We worked around and through Nancy's affair, and by November of the same year, we would be expecting our third child.

Sadly, I could not forgive or forget the news of that awful night. I could not understand or was never given a reason as to the big question of *why*. It was not until many years later, through wisdom and maturity, that I would know what questions I should have asked. Also, I was void of the gift and power of forgiveness; and soon, with the destructive forces of not forgiving, our nine years of marriage bitterly ended in a divorce.

My mom, bewildered by Nancy's actions, asked me one time, "I don't understand why a woman would give up so much in leaving her three kids."

I took a deep breath and said, "I don't know, Mom. But what I do know is there is no such thing as a no-fault divorce, so I do take some responsibility. As for her wanting to leave the kids, I don't know. What I am 100 percent sure of is I wanted and fought for our kids as they truly are the treasure created in our marriage."

As we were going through our divorce, Nancy, true to her wishes, said the only thing she wanted was the car, her clothes, and birth control and immediately moved in with the man she had just met a few months earlier.

For me, I was lucky enough to be introduced to Bill, who was an outstanding criminal attorney who took my case. I was granted full custody of the three kids, and by coincidence, Bill also had custody of his child. So we both had a bonding connection.

Soon after the divorce, Nancy got into drugs, and her visitations were rare. Rarer yet was me granting reasonable visitation, as was called out in the divorce decree.

Sad, ugly, and worse yet, with Nancy's continuous reckless actions, I did what I had to do to protect the kids. In doing so, many years later, I saw firsthand the kids' emotional scars and collateral damage, suffered from a volatile divorce. This was all caused by our human emotions running amok from the loss of someone I deeply loved.

One day, in dealing with the continued insanity, I confessed jokingly out of frustration to Bill, who had now become a close friend, "You know, I am so grateful you are also a criminal attorney. If I ever go too far and I end up killing Nancy, not only do you understand her craziness, but you can still be my attorney!"

It was my first Christmas after the divorce, and I was now in the sales department. My former manager and now Dirk's manager, Richard, invited me to his annual Christmas party at his house. I was leaving my two boys with my parents; and Mary, now three years old, was not feeling well and wanted to be with me.

I arrived at the party, holding Mary, and Tami immediately came up and took her.

Grateful, I said, "Thank you, Tami. She is not feeling well, but I just wanted to stop by, pay my respects, and wish everybody a Merry Christmas."

Tami, holding Mary tightly, said in a sweet, upbeat voice, "I'll be over here, and she'll be just fine!

As I mingled around, talking to my former workmates, I would occasionally steal a glance to check on Mary as she rested peacefully in Tami's embrace. I remember making eye contact a few times with Tami. What I instinctively noticed was the pure love and compassion that she had for kids.

As I was working full-time and taking care of the kids after work, I realized it was a godsend that both my parents were there to help. Dating was the last thing on my mind. After waiting a year, I was introduced to Georgia, a mother of five children. She was kind and a good mom, and we tried to make a go of it. But sadly, it didn't work out because I was still hurting and scared. I think of Georgia often, wondering how her life had turned out, as she also was a victim of rape.

Waiting yet another year, I dated a girl named Tina. She had two very young children and was barely able to make ends meet. It was then that I gained a whole new respect for single moms and the unfairness of having the same responsibilities yet quite a different pay scale. Sadly, we both realized that our relationship was just not going to work out, and we parted ways.

Giving up, I put it into God's hands, grateful that I had the children.

Arriving early to work, I was alone in the conference room when Dirk walked in, carrying a note. He handed it to me, grinning. "Tami told me to give this to you."

I laughed. "I am almost afraid to open it!"

Chuckling, Dirk said, "It is just an invite for you and your kids to a pool party. Oh…and Tami wants you to meet one of her friends, Tara!"

Nodding my head, I said, "We would be honored to be there, and thank you two for thinking of us."

As I was single, I did a lot of stupid things and then some. Arriving with my three kids, I brought a few bottles of Perrier water. To me, it is what I liked, but to others, it seemed snobbish. And they were right. The respectful thing to have done was to graciously drink whatever the hosts (Greg and Linnea) offered. To add insult to injury, they were also Tami and Dirk's best friends and next-door neighbors.

Tami, Dirk, and Catherine were already in the pool with Greg and Linnea's kids. Tami hollered out to my kids—James, Peter, and Mary—to come and join them. Talking to Greg and Linnea, I enjoyed watching everyone having a good time, playing in the pool. Thinking back, I remember Tami feeling conscious about her weight; she never got out of the pool until everyone was ready to eat.

After I waited nervously, it was all for naught as Tara never showed up. We thanked everyone for a wonderful time, then left.

A month passed, and I never gave Tami's friend another thought. That was until Dirk again brought me a note and explained,

"Apparently, the night Tara was supposed to meet you, she got together with her boyfriend again, but it didn't work out. If you feel like calling her, here is her number."

Grinning, I said, "This sounds like the work of Tami the matchmaker!"

Dirk, busted, smiled. "It is. But she thinks you are a pretty good guy, and she is trying to help you find someone."

Nodding my head, I said, "I understand, and that is very kind of her. Thank you, and also thank Tami."

After waiting a few days, I finally called Tara. Talking, she immediately apologized for standing me up and explained the problems and drama with her last suitor. After talking on the phone a few more times, I agreed to help her hang wallpaper in her daughter's room. Coincidently, her daughter was the same age as Mary. After dating a month, we became intimate. When I met her parents, I thought they were very nice people, and our relationship continued to grow deeper.

I don't know what it was, but I always felt there was something not quite right as it seemed Tara always had problems with men in general. When we had the opportunity to spend the night, after getting into bed, the conversation soon turned into her laying out various unnegotiable rules on what she would and would not allow sexually.

I was listening in shock. My mind was soon made up. I thought, *If this is the preamble of the hard rules set in stone for just dating, I'm not going to stick around to find out what other rules are waiting after we get married.*

I got out of bed and got dressed. Sadly, I said that I was "sorry, but this was just not going to work out" and said goodbye. Not wanting to repeat the past, I thought, *I'm not going to get remarried only to again go through another divorce. The kids have suffered enough just going through the first divorce.*

On the drive home, I adjusted my course. I was now more determined than ever. I committed myself to finishing raising my three kids. This was my life, and I was done with dating.

9

The next year brought a tremendous once-in-a-lifetime opportunity for me. Richard Bullock was leaving the company, and immediately I was offered his position as service manager. It was such a gift. I was returning to the department that I loved so much and got to interface with Dirk more often concerning all things pertaining to electronic maintenance.

With the selling of a new and very large electronic display, Dirk and Tami, to earn extra money, worked at home at night, soldering circuit boards. They would work into the very late evenings. One night, with Catherine having long been put to bed, their talk soon turned to the topic of what would happen if one of them passed away. Growing very tired, Dirk and Tami decided to wrap things up and get some much-needed sleep. As they walked down the hallway, Dirk suddenly stopped. In a mystical *Field of Dreams* moment, Dirk gently held Tami with both hands and turned to her. Looking deep into her eyes, he said, "If anything ever happens to me, a man will call you, and he won't even know why."

A hard worker, Dirk was always in demand. After finishing the large display and circuit boards, he was soon involved in another color-message project. It was through no fault of his own, but from the start, it was an abomination and was not going well in all facets—from software to hardware to total unreliability. Working many hours overtime, the sales department was working on a very large sale to a foreign country. For all involved, the pressure and stakes were unbearably high.

Late one afternoon, Tami stopped in to see if Dirk was around, worried. She had tried several times to reach him on his radio phone but was unsuccessful. I was shocked to see her as she was heavier than I had ever seen her before, and her bubbly, joking character was consumed by something deeply bothering her. When Tami left, she looked as though she was also carrying an overwhelming amount of mental weight. I still carry the memory of that day, and I will never forget it.

Getting somewhat of a vacation break, Dirk was to take the project's small prototype sample unit, which they had been tirelessly working on, to Disneyland for national televised fund-raising event.

Dirk had performed this duty many times before but always had a reliable and fully proven unit. These getaways were also an opportunity to provide his family a vacation at the company's expense.

To say the least, the message board that was supposed to constantly display the amount of donated money only worked about 50 percent of the time.

Dirk, a very conscientious man, was not only embarrassed but also deeply ashamed of letting down the people he had worked with for so many years.

As for Catherine, Tami, trying to shield her from the stress her father was going through, made the best of it even though she was also hurting for her husband's frustrations in not only dealing with the problematic unit but also not being able to spend any time with his family.

Dirk, exhausted, returned to Vegas to continue working on the problem-plagued units.

During the proceeding weekend, the family drove up to Utah to celebrate Father's Day. With stress so high, Dirk commented to Tami several times during the trip, "I just want to go home."

After returning home, Dirk resumed his stressful duties and was also going to be on call over the weekend.

For several weeks, the side window of their van remained broken. Tami, now involved with a family emergency, offered to help drive her cousins from Las Vegas to Brian Head, Utah. Angry at Dirk, she lost her temper and yelled at him as he wrapped Visqueen around the door window to seal it from the desert heat. Tami got into the car with Catherine and her cousins and drove away.

With me also being on call, I would screen the service calls as to which ones could wait and which ones I had to send someone out to repair. I got an electronic service call around 3:00 PM and spoke to Dirk as it was an easy call that shouldn't take much of his time.

Tami was now in the hotel room provided by her cousin who also managed the hotel. He made sure her room had a spa. Relaxing in the spa, Tami called Dirk in the early evening, apologizing for losing her temper. She begged him to drive up so they could spend the night together. After agreeing, he told her he would leave shortly.

It was getting late, and Tami began to worry. She could not contact Dirk with a radio phone. After waiting another hour, she went down to the front desk to talk to her cousin. Glancing out to the parking lot, she saw a car approaching. Excited and relieved, she exclaimed, "THERE'S DIRK!" As she watched the car getting closer, the reflective insignia tape on it, unreadable, flashed. Tami, somehow knowing something wasn't right, moved to the couch facing the door and sat down. As an officer walked in, their eyes met. Tami was shaking her head, with each word getting louder in denial: "No, no, no." The officer sat down, took a moment, and softly spoke, "Are you Tami Maw?"

Starting to cry, she whimpered, "Yes" as that was all she could manage to say.

The officer, choosing his words the best he could, told Tami the horrifying truth that Dirk had been killed in a car accident.

I will forever remember June 24, 1990, and the 4:00 AM phone call from Tami. I picked up the phone and said hello. Hearing Tami's shaken voice, I could immediately tell something was wrong as she began to talk.

"Hi, Gary. I need to tell you that Dirk has been killed in an accident, in the company car."

I can't remember what I said as I was shaken and also in shock, but I did manage to say something.

Tami continued, "The officer said that Dirk apparently fell asleep while driving up to Brian Head and ran into the back of a slow-moving semitruck. They also said Dirk wasn't wearing a seat belt, but he always wore a seat belt… So I don't know if it is really him."

Very sad and still in shock, I responded, "Tami, I am very sorry. Let me know whatever you need me to do for you. We are here to help."

Hanging up the phone, I was confused from Tami's last comment. I called Utah Highway Patrol, having the knowledge already of the accident, and told them the driver's name involved and the company's name who owned the vehicle. They confirmed that Dirk was killed in the accident. Not only was it one of the saddest days of my life. It now also became a double-negative day. Venturing out, I was still thinking of Dirk, Tami, and Catherine. I took the kids shopping to buy their mom a present as her birthday was the next day.

After a few days, I traveled to Utah to retrieve Dirk's computer. Reaching into the back seat for it, I noticed a few empty grape-drink bottles. I took a deep breath and played the "should've, would've, could've" game in my mind. I thought, *If he had only drank something with caffeine to help him stay awake.* It wasn't until later that I learned from Tami that they quit drinking their favorite caffeinated cold drink as part of their recommitment to their faith.

The funeral was held in Plain City, and she remained strong until the end. With the closing of the casket, realizing the finality, Tami let out a loud guttural cry that can only come from a broken woman. It echoed throughout the church.

A few months earlier, Tami had a nightmare involving a white hearse. Waking up, she immediately dismissed the nightmare as the hearses that the funeral home the family used were all gold. As she slowly followed the casket to the hearse, she realized the dream suddenly became reality as this was the first funeral using the mortuary's new white hearse.

Driving to the gravesite, Tami's sisters and their husbands sat close, held hands, and comforted each other. Tami took a deep breath. She was twenty-eight years old and now a widow and a single mother. She knew that, sadly, her world had changed.

Going to church was also unbearable. Sitting alone with Catherine as sacrament was being blessed, she noticed the husbands and wives would cuddle closer to receive the sacramental offerings of Christ. For all, it is a very special and spiritual moment. For Tami, the message of grace was passionately understood, but the sacrament was a reminder of her loneliness from losing the love of her life.

❧ **10** ❧

Returning back to Las Vegas, Tami had arranged to have a memorial for Dirk.

Most, if not all, of the company employees were in attendance, and I chose to sit in the second row. Thinking back, I can't remember who spoke or what any of their eulogies addressed, but I do remember hers.

Tami walked up to the elevated stage in front of the church; the pulpit would not do. Attached to the microphone was a long cord. Grasping it, she cradled it as if it was Dirk's heart. Standing so all could see, Tami, exposed, was totally open, allowing for her freedom of movement. Using no notes and her voice full of emotion but never breaking, she proudly stood testifying to the love she had for Dirk and shared a few funny personal stories—a fitting tribute to a wonderful husband, a loving father, and most importantly, a Christlike example of what we should all strive to be.

Watching her, I was in awe. Inside my mind, I was shaking my head as I was totally encapsulated by her unbelievable strength and courage. So pure, so honest, and such a strong and loving woman. I could only think of Dirk looking down and how blessed he must have felt. As for me, I was the luckiest man to witness what true love was, which, for the longest time, had eluded me.

As it was the day before a holiday, I had to go back to work, so I did not have a chance to talk to Tami. After getting off work, I went home first before I had to go and pick up the kids. I picked up the phone. I felt I needed to call her. I dialed the number I had just dialed nine days earlier, and it was answered by a soft female voice. I asked for Tami, and the voice replied, "Tami is resting right now."

I replied, "I understand. Could you tell her Gary called?"

I heard Tami's distant voice in the background say, "Mom, who is it?"

The voice softly answered, "It's Gary."

"Mom, it's okay. I'll take it."

I heard the noise of the phone changing hands, and in a very tired voice, Tami said, "Hi, Gary. I saw you at the memorial service."

Stumbling for words, I softly said, "I don't know why I am calling…but I just felt I should."

I have no idea what I said after that or how long the call was. But I am glad I made the call.

Hanging up, Tami shook her head over the prophesized words Dirk had spoken many months before, and she teasingly thought, *Dirk, not Gary!*

As Tami was selling their Las Vegas home, she was already building a new house in Utah. The contactor learned that she had just lost her husband, so he put a concerted effort and finished it in thirty days.

Tami, returning to Vegas to sign the final closing paperwork, stopped by to visit with Dirk's coworkers. Making a concerted effort to say hi to me, Tami wished me an early Happy Birthday. We talked for a few minutes. She asked about the kids, and she told me about her new house. As we were still good friends, she wanted to stay in touch and gave me her new phone number.

Looking back now, I realize how easy it is, using the current technology when starting up a relationship. Trying by sheer luck to visit each other over a landline phone had its extreme and inconvenient limitations.

During a few of our earlier phone conversations, Tami told me she was not doing well at night; now that she was sleeping alone, she almost never got any sleep.

To help her out during the day in performing the manly things that needed to be done in a new house, she enlisted help from Dave (who was Steve's brother) and her old high school friend. Still at home, living with his mom, Dave did everything he could to be her next husband. This also included a few brief physical encounters.

During a few of our evening phone calls and with Dave at Tami's, in the TV room, Tami would put a blanket over herself as she talked to me. One particular night on the phone, I asked if she would travel down to Vegas and said I would fix dinner. She quickly and eagerly accepted.

With Tami having so much family close by, Catherine loved the chance to spend playtime with her many cousins. This gave Tami the opportunity to take a break from being a young widowed mom.

Arriving, she looked so beautiful. Sitting on the barstool in the kitchen, she watched me as I prepared a gourmet dinner. Tami, the consummate trooper, not liking mushrooms, remained quiet as she ate just a few as we visited.

Finished, we retired to the living room, where I started a fire before we sat down on the couch. As I had a very stressful day, Tami offered to message my head as I lay down in her lap. Within minutes, I could feel her fingers pulling the stress out of my body.

Having the gift of remembering very important dates that forever changed my life, I can say September 21 was the most important day in my life, and I could never turn it back. As we embraced, friendship transcended into a relationship. Her clothes tenderly fell around her, and I could hear my heart as we softy, tenderly, and lovingly became one.

I was never motivated by pity for Tami in her loss of Dirk. What did motivate me were her soul and spirit, which impassioned me to love her more than I did the day before.

I believed that if I hurt her by breaking up, I would be the worst person ever to be born on this planet and would self-condemn my spirit on Judgment Day.

After Tami left, she later told me she went to a fast-food restaurant and, after going into the bathroom, cried. She was fearful that what had just happened, which appeared to be so true, would somehow not last as she felt she had surrendered herself too fast. Confused and worried, Tami surmised I would selfishly disavow the night as a one-night stand, and she would be quickly forgotten.

Going to bed that night, I peacefully lay down and thought of my feelings and what she must be feeling and going through. I was also questioning myself concerning my actions as Dirk's passing had only been eighty-nine days ago. I did, however, know one thing for certain. It was Tami's soul and spirit that had always attracted me to her for a long time.

Waking up the next morning, I felt a warmth burning inside my once deeply bruised heart. I was changed. It was as if the soft rays of hope had awakened and stirred my soul.

Getting up, I quickly called Greg and Linnea's house to get their address and talk to Tami. Both of us were cheerful and upbeat. We talked measuredly as we carefully nurtured our deepening friendship for each other.

Later that day, Tami received the flowers I sent her, which greatly relieved her fears from the previous night.

11

During the next week, we talked continuously every day on the phone. Excited, I was looking forward to Tami spending Saturday night with me. As she was arriving, I again was fixing dinner for her, and the mood and atmosphere were much more relaxed. Finished, we went for a scenic drive.

The one thing I noticed right away that I loved was the ease of conversing with her and the subject matter she discussed as I listened.

The one word she asked that I would never use was the *F* word.

Understanding, I said, "I will try to never use it in front of you, but if you stop by my work, all bets are off."

Tami, giggling, said, "No not *that F* word. The word *fat*. I prefer the word to reference my weight to be *fluffy*!"

Laughing and smiling, I said, "I promise!"

After returning home, I started a fire in the fireplace. I held her as we continued to visit on the couch. As the crackling roar of the fire slowly died, turning into softly glowing embers, we both grew more quiet and tired. I took her hand, and we rose from the couch. Then we walked into the bedroom. We got undressed, then slowly made love. As we were resting, holding each other, we both peacefully fell asleep.

As dawn slowly approached, I was still blissfully sleeping. Little did I know, Tami had woken up as the first rays of sunlight pierced the bedroom. She was lying in bed, fearful not about us but how was she going to touch up her hair and makeup and then crawl back in bed without awakening me! Whatever she did, she managed to pull it off and confessed a few months later, to my amusement.

A few weeks later, Tami again spent the weekend with me. Much to my parents' concern, they instinctively knew something was going on. When I took her over to meet them, it went very well. Kind, gentle, and respectful, she knew that both of my parents were also very involved with the kids, and she thought very highly of them for being such a big and helpful part as grandparents in the family.

As we were planning our first coming-out event, we just happened to be at a Jewish wedding. Attending, we were aware that there would be people that we both knew from work. What did come as a surprise to both of us was their reactions. Finding two open seats, we sat behind the daughter of our general manager. She glanced back at me and smiled. Then she gave a courteous nod. Just then, in the corner of her eye, she caught sight of Tami. When she contorted her head, I swear we both thought we heard her neck snap! The most beautiful thing was that we felt at ease and happy as we both complemented each other.

Ecstatic for Tami and I to be together, in the interim, I had a heated discussion over the phone with Nancy. With the kids at my parents' for the weekend, I was looking forward to spending time with Tami and enjoying her love, compassion, and company.

As we sat together at home, I was still stressed over my fight with Nancy and felt the need to take a break. I asked, "You feel like taking a walk?"

Despite feeling happy and upbeat, she could tell something was just not right. "Sure. Have I done something wrong?"

I smiled as I shook my head. "*Oh, heavens, no!* I love spending every bit of my time with you!"

Holding hands, we walked for a bit as I remained quiet. Tami, both wise and patient, instinctively waited for me to open up.

Finally ready, in a calm voice, I said, "I had a heated discussion this afternoon with Nancy."

In a gentle voice, she replied, "Oh! From how you're acting, I figured she had something to do with it. I am sorry she upset you."

Turning and smiling, I said, "Thank you, and I am *so* happy you're here. Yes, she did upset me. But the sad thing is it wasn't about visitation. It was about crazy, stupid stuff in the past that doesn't apply or matter anymore."

I stopped, turned, and grasped both of Tami's hands, then lovingly looked deep into her eyes. "Please take what I am about to say, and please don't get upset. I don't want to diminish what you are going through as it is more than I can ever imagine. I know your pain is so crushing from the loss of Dirk. But as painful as it is, your grief is real. But there is one thing for certain. In its horrible finality, it's over. The love and memories you two shared, you will always have. Tragically, the part you will never get over is that you two were robbed of your future, like Dirk not being able to see Catherine grow into becoming an adult, Catherine getting married, and you two getting to be grandparents. I am so sorry.

"In my situation of being divorced, I am slowly coming to the realization that there is no end. Thinking today while driving home, I realized Nancy is like a temperamental toilet spewing its vile waste, and no matter what you do, there is not a plumber on Earth that can fix it."

Tami giggling, "Gary I am not laughing at you. I am laughing as that was quite a descriptive metaphor! And no, I do not take offence, and everything you said is true."

We embraced and kissed, then we held hands again. We walked home for a romantic and peaceful night.

In years past, as I was a single father, during the Christmas season, I sought refuge in "the Happiest Place on Earth." With Christmas a few months away, I invited Tami and Catherine to join us in driving down to Disneyland. I thought it would be good therapy for Tami and Catherine, and it would also be a great place to start blending our families together. I also thought it would also help them get through the holiday season, as it did for me the many years of being a single father.

Our Disneyland getaway weekend finally arrived. James walked to the gate while the rest of us stayed in the car as he wanted to be the first in line. Succeeding was no problem as the temperature was about thirty-nine degrees, and the crowds were sparse.

As we walked onto Main Street, the Christmas decorations took my breath away (they always did), and I was so happy to see Tami and Catherine getting so excited. My goal was complete, but little did I know that Tami's goal was something completely different.

Spending two days at Disneyland, we did everything. Looking back, with all the kids getting along so well and having fun, like a typical man, I was letting important events pass while I concentrated on my goal.

What I should have been doing was holding Tami's hand more often and every once in a while surprising her with a kiss. I know. Men are stupid.

We were soon going to leave Disneyland. On our final night, I went to my hotel room with the boys, and Tami went to her room with the girls, which left us no time to spend time together and share our feelings.

We were leaving the hotel in the morning to drive back to Vegas, and soon Tami began crying. I never sensed it, nor did she ever say it. But deep down inside, she was hoping I would *propose to her* with the kids witnessing it while at Disneyland.

By the time we got to Vegas, I asked Tami and Catherine if they would like to spend Christmas with us, which she happily agreed to.

We spent Christmas as a family, Tami and I were so happy, and it felt so right with both us and the kids.

A couple of days after Christmas, Tami left to go back to Utah to drop off Catherine and drive back as we wanted to spend New Year's Eve together.

Tami returned in the early afternoon on New Year's Eve, and my parents took the kids.

Sitting on the couch, waiting for midnight, Tami broached the subject of marriage. "Gary, I really enjoyed going to Disneyland, and everybody got along so well. I know you are scared to get married again, and I understand. For me, I was happily married, and I want to be happily married again…to you."

I nodded my head. "I love you, Tami, and I want to be with you forever."

We were passionately kissing and holding each other when Tami hurriedly broached, "What date were you thinking?"

I pondered for a moment, and a flash memory came to me. I grabbed Tami's hand and said, "I don't know, but the boys have a *The Simpsons* calendar in their bedroom. Let's go look at it!"

Thumbing through the months, we suddenly came to May. I paused and teased, "Well, your birthday is on April 4, and May 4 is on a Saturday. What do you think?"

Tami, smiling as she nodded her head, giggled. "And May 4, according to *The Simpsons*, is Lumpy Rug Day, so we can't go wrong with that!"

Little did we know that our wedding date years later (thanks to the *Star Wars* film series) would famously be addressed as "May the 4th be with you!"

Celebrating midnight, we brought in 1991: In love, engaged, happy, and soon a married blended family.

❦ **12** ❦

We spent the rest of the New Year's week together, and Tami expanded into her new role of being a mother to my three kids. They thought she was pretty cool and liked her a lot. With that, they quickly became hers too. Mary, the youngest of the three, when I divorced, never knew much about having a mom. With the boys playing outside, Mary, unsure and a little scared, innocently asked, "Are you going to leave me like my first mommy?"

So touched by such a sincere and innocent question, Tami gave Mary a reassuring smile. She tenderly picked her up and held her tight. Making eye contact, Tami lovingly spoke, "Mary, I promise I will never leave you or the boys. I want to be your mommy… forever."

After dropping the kids off at my parents', we headed up to Utah for the weekend so I could ask Tami's dad for permission to marry her. It was our first road trip together with just her and me, and we enjoyed visiting and talking about the future!

After arriving at Tami's house, she took time to give me a tour. It was beautifully decorated. I was impressed with her skills in transforming it into a very nice home. Having just enough time, we freshened up and changed our clothes before heading down to her parents.

Not knowing what to expect, walking into their house, I was greeted first by Imara. I also met Bob. We sat at their small dining room table. Engaged in small talk, both Imara and Bob wanted to get to know as much as they could about me in the short time they had.

I finished addressing my brief history of life and cut to the chase with no memorized script. "Bob, I have come up here to tell you that I love your daughter very much. I also feel it is also a matter of deep respect to Imara and Tami. I am here to ask your blessing in marrying your daughter."

Bob glanced over at Imara. Her eyes were gleaming. He then glanced over to Tami, who was brightly smiling. After taking a few minutes, Bob turned to me and smiled as he nodded his head. "You have my blessing!"

Standing up, I said, "Thank you, Bob and Imara. You both raised a wonderful daughter."

Grabbing Tami, I gave her a passionate and grateful kiss.

Before long, the whole house was filled to standing room only with Tami's sisters and their families. I was overwhelmed; there were so many names to try to remember as well as who belonged to who. And to add to the chaos, everybody talked at once. One child I did know was Catherine, and I spent a few minutes catching up with her.

As the night wore on and the relatives thinned out, we left with Catherine and went back to Tami's house. Getting Catherine ready for bed, Tami called out to me. I walked into Catherine's room and knelt down by her bed as my future wife stood behind me.

In a very soft, loving voice, as I sought a positive answer from a child I knew was still coping and hurting from the loss of her dad, I gently asked, "Catherine, I asked your grandpa tonight if I could marry your mom, and he gave us his blessing. But I am here now, asking you the same question. Can I have your blessing for me to marry your mom?"

Catherine, nonemotional but supportive of her mom in wanting to see her happy, softly replied, "Yes."

I stayed over the weekend, and a few more family gatherings were held. Tami had told her sisters that I looked like Kevin Costner. No matter how long I stood in front of a mirror, wishing…I would never ever come close!

With the family being so involved in church, taking matters into her own hands, Tami haphazardly solved it. Coming up with a plan unknown to me, she created a fake marriage certificate and presented it to her parents to put them at ease. They, in turn, would pass the news on to the sisters.

The ruse encapsulated us as we went to the justice of peace first thing in the morning and got married, all before traveling to Utah. In addition, we were still going to have a wedding ceremony on May 4 as a celebration for all our friends and relatives to enjoy. Eventually, it never really fooled anyone, but kudos to Tami as it was quite a creative cover!

I boarded a plane late Sunday afternoon. Tami stayed behind and, with the assistance of the three brothers-in-law, loaded the moving truck bound for Las Vegas.

Tami arrived a week later with Peter accompanying her. Catherine remained in school until Tami could register her in Las Vegas. On Catherine's arrival in Vegas, the principal put her in James's class since they were in the same grade, and it would also help Catherine have a smoother transition.

Finally all together, we officially began blending our family on January 15, 1991.

Within a few weeks, lying in bed, we were discussing what type of wedding rings we liked. For me, this would be something new; since I was working with electricity, I gave Nancy a pass on purchasing one for me.

Knowing exactly what she wanted, Tami expressed she wanted a Marquise-cut center diamond. I agreed and told her what diamond jeweler to go to as I had sold him a sign and we were good friends.

The next morning, while I was at work, Tami went to see the jeweler and picked out my ring, and I was to stop by after I got off work to see which one she had picked out.

Walking into the jewelry store, I was happy to see my friend. "Hey, Lou, how have you been?"

Lou was upbeat and cheerful. "Really good, Gary. I guess Tami told you she was in earlier this morning."

Nodding my head, I smiled. "Yes! Tami also said she picked out my ring and wanted me to approve it."

Lou briefly went into the back portion of his shop and returned. He opened the small velvet ring box, then handed it to me.

I was stunned. "Lou, how much does this cost?"

Lou shot me a quick glance. "This ring sells for six hundred dollars."

I took it all in, pausing for a moment, then I spoke, "Tami said she picked out a few rings for her. Could you show me them?"

Lou, upbeat, led me to the women's wedding ring display and pulled one out. He exclaimed, "Tami really liked this one!" as he handed the ring. It sparkled even when it was still encased in the box.

I was almost afraid to ask. In my mind, I had a rough idea of how much I thought it cost as I cautiously quizzed, "Lou, how much is this one?"

Lou, keeping his eyes focused on the display case, said in a relaxed, easy tone, "This one is $650."

Looking up at Lou, I said, "Lou, these two rings cost a lot more than what you are quoting me. Did Tami put you up to this!"

Lou, somewhere along the borderline of amusement and embarrassment, smiled and confessed, "You are right. But that's what Tami really wants."

Nodding my head, I smiled. "Lou, can you show me what you have in a Marquise cut?"

Lou, obliging, pulled out several rings, finding one that was similar to what she had picked out but more in line with my budget. That was the one I picked for Tami.

Lou got my ring size, and within a week, Tami picked them up.

Tami and I went to our favorite restaurant, and after finishing our dinner in a secluded booth, we helped each other put on our rings. We embraced and kissed as we were both very happy with our choices.

✶✶✶✶✶

With less than four months to prepare for the wedding, we had the garage remodeled, turning it into a big bedroom for the boys. The girls each had a bedroom, and Tami and I got the master bedroom.

With Tami working her decorating magic on the interior, I started changing the dirt backyard into a lush Japanese garden landscape by first building a koi fishpond.

With everybody working hard, miraculously, we finished 95 percent of our projects on April 4—just in time for Tami's birthday.

For the remainder of the time until the wedding date, Tami had her parents come down. As she and her mom hung drapes, I was told to keep Bob busy as I still had to put the outdoor lighting in the backyard.

On the morning of May 4, the weather could not have been better. We were living in an eight-house cul-de-sac, and all the neighbors were invited. The chairs and tables were set up in the middle of the street. The caterer arrived with his large smoker and open trailer to prepare the dinner. In the backyard, the folding chairs were set up on the patio and lawn area.

Tami, in the early afternoon, left with her parents to go have her hair and makeup done. With all my assignments finished, everything looked so beautiful as I stood across the street, talking with my neighbor and also my best man, Don. Seeing Tami returning with her parents brought a loving smile to my face and a warm feeling in my heart. Quickly waving, she tried keeping the custom of the groom not seeing the bride until she walked down the aisle. After getting out of the car, she quickly disappeared into the house.

With all the guest seated, James, Peter, my best man, our next-door neighbor Preacher Tom, and I stood on our rehearsed spots as we patiently waited for the moment to begin.

Little did I know until years later that Tami was experiencing a moment of indecision and second-guessing. She was all dressed and holding her bouquet. Imara took a picture of her standing in front of the bathroom mirror as she starred deeply into it. Perhaps she was waiting for an epiphany of approval from Dirk. Or perhaps she was taking a few moments to reflect.

Ready, syncing her mind with her heart, she closed the door on her past and opened the door to a second marriage and her life ahead.

Imara took a few minutes and emerged to announce that the beads in Tami's hat had gotten stuck in the netting of the wedding dress and that she would be out momentarily.

Hearing the music starting, Catherine, Mary, and the bride's attendants walked down the grass aisle to their assigned spots.

Preacher Tom, on seeing Tami and her dad, announced, "Will all the guests please stand!"

With everyone rising, Tami looked so beautiful as she and her dad walked toward us.

With all the guest seated, Preacher Tom in his booming voice asked, "Who giveth this woman to be married to this man?"

Even though this was a non-LDS wedding, a Temple wedding was a family expectation and was achieved with all of the four daughters. Given this opportunity in a traditional wedding, it was Bob's one and only chance to announce, "I do! On a no-deposit, no-return basis."

When the crowd's laughter subsided, the wedding began.

Reading from Tami's and my own prepared words, Preacher Tom also included the words and actions of Jesus Christ and God.

Soon the moment arrived. Pastor Tom asked us to turn and face each other. We stood close and held each other's hands, and our eyes gleamed as we listened to the vows and answered attentively.

We were waiting for the words we both longed for, then Pastor Tom announced with great joy, "Gary and Tami, I now pronounce you man and wife. You may now kiss the bride!"

As we were embracing, I both pleasantly surprised and shocked Tami by French-kissing her. No peck on the lips would suffice in this beautiful, momentous, and loving occasion.

Adlibbing, all *our* kids came over, and we all hugged as we began our journey…together.

—◌ 13 ◌—

Tami had never been to San Diego, and as we were newlyweds, we were kid-free for three days. We stayed at a new hotel located on the beach. Our room overlooked the pool and Jacuzzi, with the Pacific Ocean as a background. The resort was truly a romantic honeymoon spot filled with many encapsulating and precious moments during our honeymoon. Returning for future visits only added to a lifetime of precious memories.

One of Tami's most breathtaking moments was at Point Loma Lighthouse. We were standing together at the point overlooking San Diego, Coronado Island, and the Pacific Ocean.

This was the first lighthouse Tami had ever seen and was located in such a unique place. Gazing and overwhelmed, she slowly turned her head from left to right in awe and exclaimed, "I love this! Such a quiet, beautifully isolated place! I have never seen anything like this before in my life. To be able to have such a panoramic view... This is truly breathtaking."

Tami was like a child on Christmas morning, excited to see the prized gift she told Santa she wanted. She pointing and shrieked, "Look at the sailboats! There are so many of them!"

Holding each other tightly, we watched them as they tacked back and forth. Breaking her silence, Tami innocently surmised, "They look like floating white butterflies with their wings folded up!"

With the lighthouse in the background, we embraced, and I kissed her. As we were hugging, I whispered into her ear, "I love you so much, and I want to spend the rest of my life with you."

Walking together, we went to an overlook. Deep in thought somewhere between her past, our present, and the future, she gazed out over the Pacific Ocean as the sun was setting. Chasing the ever-diminishing light and colors, I quickly took a silhouette picture, capturing the moment.

One can only wonder what she was thinking. At every sunset, we paused to witness and reflect another ending day of our life. For others, a sunrise awakens them with the promise of hope and the birth and opportunity of a new day.

One of our most cherished honeymoon memories happened late one night. I wanted Tami, so I woke her up and teasingly whispered, "Want to go out to the balcony and make love?"

Her voice, sure but also unsure, exclaimed, "Somebody might see us!"

I giggled. "They might, or they might not. Besides, it's secluded enough!"

She thought for a moment before jumping out of bed. She challenged, "Race you to see who gets undressed first!"

I giggled again. "I'll let you win. I like the view!"

As we held hands, I guided her out onto our concealed hotel balcony. Embracing, kissing, and slowly letting ourselves go, we soon enveloped into a loving encounter. With nature providing the white noise, together we embraced as one. We listened to the waves as they tenderly teased and caressed the shoreline.

Arriving on the fourth day, Tami's parents brought our kids. Together we revisited a few of the places Tami and I had already been to.

To give the kids a treat and everlasting memories, we also went to the San Diego Zoo and SeaWorld.

We went to restaurant on Harbor Island where the kids were treated to their first lobster. Tami was curious, so I offered her some, and she braved a taste…and liked it. From there on, if any restaurant had lobster on its bill of fare, she ordered it.

We were both in agreement. Our honeymoon/vacation truly set the foundation for us, our kids, and our ever-growing love for each other. We returned home, and our lives returned to a routine as we now began as an official blended family.

*****

I went back to work, and a month into our marriage, I decided to surprise Tami with a phone call. I listened intently, and on hearing her pick up the phone, I spoke, "Hi, my love! I just wanted to call and see how your day is going."

Tami sounded lighthearted and nonchalant. "Oh, not too eventful. I am lying on the couch, naked, eating bonbons while watching TV dramas!"

I was taken by surprise. With my imagination running wild, I tried to picture Tami's words, visualizing what this could possibly look like. I was still wrestling with creating a visualization; my mind was too overloaded to respond.

I was taking a moment to formulate a clear picture in my mind and stumbled over the only word I could come up with: "Really?"

Tami was giggling. "*Yes*, I do this every morning!"

Like a well-told joke, Tami pausing for a moment and continued, "Well, now that I have your undivided attention, *no*. I am actually doing something sexier. I am doing laundry, making beds, and doing other housework!

I laughed and said, "I wish I didn't have such a hectic day. I would love to come home and hand-feed you bonbons!"

Tami, throughout our marriage, had a system for doing housework. After I went to work and the kids were dropped off at school, she would come home and strip down naked to do the housework. While doing this, Tami had two ironclad rules: don't fry bacon, and don't clean windows. When finished, Tami would go take a shower and then get dressed.

With my first wife Nancy and I being baptized LDS, I had hoped religion would help hold our marriage together. As a family, we went to church regularly and eventually became inactive before finally divorcing. As a single father barely able to both work and take care of the kids, I remained inactive.

One of the best things Tami ever did with our family happened right after our honeymoon. She insisted we all go back to church, which was paramount to her and our family.

One of Tami's first callings was being the chorister leader. Every Sunday, I loved watching her lead the music, dressed in her glowing white dress. She looked so beautiful and happy.

The children quickly making new friends was a blessing as most of those friendships lasted all throughout school and many years after.

While married to Dirk, Tami tried her hand a few times at being a stand-up comedian. With her quick wit; brassy, unabashed, and bold attitude; and being very funny, she held her own while entertaining her audience. She took her gift of making people laugh, and she always was the person to beat during the once-a-year church talent night and always stole the show. To me, the best part was not laughing at her antics, as that was only a sideshow. The bigger show was watching her blossom and grow while enjoying her life to the fullest.

While we were still in the honeymoon period of our marriage, one morning, Tami received a surprise call from Nancy.

Tami remained silent to both me and the kids. She patiently waited for the kids to go to bed.

We retired to our room, then she sat on the corner of the bed and patted the mattress with her hand, encouraging, "Gary, come and sit by me!"

After I sat, in an upbeat voice, she continued, "Nancy called this afternoon to talk to me about visiting the kids."

I shot a surprised look. "Well, I guess it was only a matter of time. What did you tell her?"

"I have invited her and her boyfriend over on Tuesday night so we can all talk. Gary, I am going to be honest. In raising our kids, if we stand in the way of having them see Nancy, years later, when the kids are teenagers, this can really come back to bite us."

I nodded my head in agreement. "We have only been married a few months, and you know what I like best about you?"

She shot a surprised yet suspicious look. "What?"

I put the Cheshire cat to shame with my smile and giggled. "You always being right!"

As I sat outside on our backyard patio, the doorbell rang. I heard Tami open the door, and I could hear her and Nancy talking as the voices grew louder. Facing the patio door, I could see Nancy carrying a stack of legal folders.

Taking a deep breath, I surmised, *This is going to be an interesting evening.* Just then, her boyfriend stepped out from behind Nancy. I finished my thought: *I was wrong. It's going to be a very interesting evening.*

I closed the patio door, and Tami was speaking in a pleasant, encouraging voice. "Nancy, go ahead and sit here, and, Louis, you sit here next to Nancy."

When all were seated, Tami, in a soft, pleasant voice, spoke, "Thank you, Nancy and Louis, for coming over tonight. Nancy, in our phone call, I briefly touched on establishing a visitation schedule."

Nancy cut off Tami, wrestling her folders and quickly pulling one out. "Tami, I want to get a few things straight with you on my past visitations and Gary being such a jerk."

Immediately cutting Nancy off in a stern, commanding voice, Tami retorted, "Nancy, *that* is in the past. What I want *now* is for *you* to have visitation every other weekend. When you come to pick up the kids, you are to come into our house and visit for a while. *Gary*, you are to be cordial and accommodating to Nancy. Nancy, when you return with the kids, you are to again come in and visit, and again, Gary, you are to be nice to Nancy. Gary, in the past, you had the kids wait at the curb, and, Nancy, you were instructed to drop the kids off at the curb. I have one thing to say about that. Our children are not trash that we leave and pick up on the curb. We will *all* get along from this day forward in the interest of the children."

Sitting and watching Tami, I was awestruck by both her power and her wisdom. Most of all, she was right. The battle and war had gone on for too long, and it needed to end.

Tami sat down, and the evening quickly developed into pleasant conversation.

The one thing I remembered Louis talking about that has stuck with me for a lifetime was his drug addiction. When asked how he was doing with his rehabilitation, he said, "It's a battle I fight every day."

Several months later, taking a summer retreat vacation, our family all went up to Bear Lake to camp out with all of Tami's family. I was not a big camping fan; my idea of roughing it consisted of going to San Diego without hotel reservations! For Tami, on the other hand, camping was in her blood, and she was good at it.

One morning, an altercation broke out between a brother-in-law and his son. It was growing hotter, and once again I got to witness Tami's skill and bravery as she interjected herself physically between both of the angry participants. In less than a minute, the arguing cooled down as she talked and reasoned with both of them, and peace was eventually restored.

Standing close by to assist Tami if needed, I got to witness a truly remarkable woman that would never cease to amaze or surprise me for the rest of my life. I was truly a blessed man.

14

As our marriage seasoned, I can't remember why Tami had to go to the airport.

Walking by one of the ticket counters, she noticed a young man about eighteen years old standing in front of a ticket agent's counter, crying.

Concerned, she stopped and gently and softly asked, "Hi. What is wrong, and what can I do to help?"

The young man, calming down enough to talk, confessed, "My grandma has passed away, and my mom was supposed to have paid for a ticket for me to pick up here. I don't know what happened, but it is not here, and my grandma's funeral is tomorrow."

Tami moved closer to the counter to speak to the agent. "Is there any way you can call his mom to get her credit card number for the ticket?"

The agent, calm and respectful, said, "I tried, but there was no answer."

Tami took a few minutes to think, then turned. She took a long look at the young man and then turned back to the agent. "How much is the ticket?"

The agent was suddenly alarmed. "Miss, can I please speak to you at the other end of the counter?"

Smiling, Tami replied, "Sure." She followed in step, parallel with the agent.

Turning to address Tami, the agent, in a concerned tone, said, "I think your kindness in wanting to help is very generous. But please, I want to caution you and be aware that there is no guarantee you will ever be paid back, and we cautiously, as a policy, are required to warn against any outside financial assistance in doing this."

Tami nodded her head and glanced back at the young man for a moment. Turning back to the agent, she cautiously spoke, "Thank you for your concern. I appreciate it. Now, how much is the ticket?"

The agent, courteous but businesslike, replied, "A one-way ticket is $334.44."

Smiling in confidence, Tami said, "I want to pay for this young man's ticket."

Both walked back. Tami presented her credit card as the agent began taking the young man's information.

While printing the ticket, the agent said in a courteous tone, "Mrs. Hendricks, here is your card back. And Mr. Russell, here is your ticket. Your gate number is B4."

Very politely the young man took the ticket, and he very respectfully asked the agent for a piece of paper and a pen. He turned to Tami. "Mrs. Hendricks, I can't thank you enough for what you have done for me. Could you please write down your name and address so my mom can send you a check?"

Tami wrote down her name and address, gave it back, and quizzed, "I know your last name. By the way, my name is Tami. What is your first name?"

"My name is John. Tami, thank you for your kindness, and I promise my mom will send you a check."

Tami hugged John. "I know you will, and I am sorry for the loss of your grandmother."

She returned home, and when I greeted my beloved wife at the door, she confessed, "I helped someone at the airport, and I hope you won't be upset."

Hugging her, I said in a reassuring voice, "I won't be upset!"

She took a few minutes before she told me her story. When she finished, she was trying to read me and questioned, "Well, what do you think?"

Smiling, I said, "I think you are a very kind person, and you *did* the right thing. I think it is going to be very interesting to see if they send you back a check, as I have my doubts."

A week later, to my amazement, the check arrived!

*****

Ten months into our marriage, this would be our first time celebrating St. Patrick's Day, which was also Dirk's birthday.

Later on that night, I had already fallen asleep when suddenly Tami, shaking me, woke me up.

As I was shaking the cobwebs out of my head, in a very emotional and loud whisper, Tami said, "I think I heard Dirk in Catherine's room!"

Skeptical and in denial, I started to speak when suddenly I also heard a noise. Both of us were now deathly quiet. We again heard another noise, and she whispered, "Gary, go see if Catherine's all right!"

We were both scared and chicken. It was not exactly my finest moment. Pulling the sheet over my head, I cowardly retorted, "He's your husband! You go deal with him!"

While we were adjusting as a blended family and as husband and wife, Tami approached me with the idea of attending an encounter group in Sacramento conducted by our friend's sister. They would also accompany us.

It was scheduled for the weekend, and it consisted of group sessions. In these groups, the counselor would then break us into smaller groups. In that final selection, Tami and I were separated. Seated, I watched from across the room as the group, standing, slowly surrounded Tami as she sat in the middle of them. The counselor, now one-on-one with my wife, started to break her down. Not able to see or hear, I was confident in the counselor's credentials. After about thirty minutes, a woman suddenly broke away from the group and quickly approached me. Upset, she blurted out, "I can't believe your wife is still in love with her first husband while being married to you."

I chose not to engage her, and she soon walked away. I was not upset with Tami, nor could I be. A marriage that ended in death is a lot different than a marriage that ended in divorce. The outcome and collateral damage are quite different.

When they were finished with Tami, it was my turn. Vicious and verbally attacking me, the counselor tried to belittle, intimidate, and insult me by speculating as to why my first wife cheated on me. She was literally getting in my face. I would not engage, which only made her madder. To say the least, my session didn't last long.

After leaving Sacramento, we flew to San Diego for a few days. San Diego, in a lot of ways, is a hospital paradise for the finding and revitalization of souls. I used to say, "If Mexico and Hawaii could have a baby, they would name it San Diego." There again without our kids, we took time to be with each other to just talk, listen, understand, grow, appreciate and most importantly…love.

Flying back to Las Vegas, rested and rejuvenated, we would soon face some of our biggest and most tender tests of our marriage.

~ **15** ~

With the kids getting a little older, Tami, wanting to be a travel agent, enrolled in a travel agency school. She was both talented and, most of all, bright. But sadly, a lot of times in our marriage, her confidence sometimes waned, and she would not believe in herself.

Not understanding, I gave her my love and support and, most of all, helped her. Tami was determined to succeed. Together we quizzed each other for her to learn the required airport codes. Throughout our marriage, I always admired her resourcefulness. She was having trouble with one airport code in particular; she could never remember Baltimore's BWI airport code. To help herself, Tami associated the letters BWI with "big women in Baltimore"! Later on in life, I can honestly say that having flown into Baltimore several times, I never saw any big women!

Some of the big perks as a travel agent was that Tami would come across some great deals. At one such time, she arranged for us to take our whole family to Hawaii. The house, just short of a mansion, was situated on a beach with a pool in the backyard. At night we would lie in bed, hold each other, and listen to the waves as we slowly fell asleep.

We returning from Hawaii and back to our daily routine. A few months later, Tami, performing her morning routine, was driving James and his friend to school. They were waiting at the busy intersection, and the light soon turned green. They ventured into the intersection, and she started her left-hand, turn unaware of a speeding car running the red light. Suddenly and violently that car T-boned into our van, crashing into the driver's side. The car was traveling so fast that its momentum violently spun the van around, emitting a tremendous noise. Just as fast as it happened, all things became quiet.

Still buckled in her seat, lifeless, Tami passed away. As her spirit left her body, she took one last look. Her spirit then started its journey as it ascended to and through the veil into heaven.

Our son's friend bolted out of the van and started screaming, "Get out! Get out! The van is going to catch on fire!" as he ran in circles around it.

James, in shock, stayed with his mom. Scared and helpless, all he could do to help was pray over her lifeless body.

Tami emerged from the veil, blanketed in total silence. Appearing before her was a sky bluer than she had ever seen. Puffy clouds emblazoned with accents of peach, cream, and purple took on an ever-changing life of their own.

Before her lay a quiet stream surrounded by flowers dazzling in bright vivid colors never seen on Earth. As they were touched by God's hand, they were even more enhanced by His purity and perfection.

Tami's spirit was comforted. She gazed at her hands and gown as both glowed exceedingly white. She followed the path along the stream, and it soon led to a group of bright-bodied souls. Softly smiling, she began to recognize that the gentle souls were her loved ones that had passed.

Seeing Dirk, she realized another heavenly sensation. Thoughts replaced words.

Oh, Dirk, how I have missed you.

Dirk smiled in a way his beloved wife had never seen before. *I have missed you too.*

Moving forward, she tenderly communicated with all of her relatives and friends for what seemed like forever.

Soon Dirk's whole body was glowing, full of love. *Tami, time here is not like on Earth. You need to go back while you still can.*

Tami was confused. *Go back? But I want to stay here!*

Gently and lovingly Dirk thought, *I know. And I understand. But you have to go back as you still have so much to do in your life, your family's life, and many others'.*

Tami, trying to understand, asked, *Is it possible to go back?*

Dirk tenderly smiled. *Yes, it is possible, but most importantly, we need you to go back to help Gary become a better person.*

Not understanding yet understanding, Tami smiled as she took one last look at her loved ones, then she was gone.

As Tami's spirit descended, she gazed at her lifeless body and saw a man frantically trying to bring her back to life. She suddenly rejoined her body, the spirit becoming a soul, and immediately she felt the tremendous human sensation of pain from the trauma inflicted on her. Tami would later tell me, "When my spirit reentered my body, it was the most painful experience that I had ever endured in my life."

Witnessing and bringing the woman come back to life was the man who ran the red light. He had fallen asleep at the wheel after a long night at work, and as he was a paramedic firefighter, he successfully used all his skills to bring her back.

Sitting at my work desk, I answered the ringing phone as a concerned voice spoke, "Gary, this is Martha at church. Tami was in an accident, and they are taking her to the county hospital. James and Christopher are okay, and we will take them home."

I quickly called my parents and asked them to go to our house and wait for all the kids to get home from school. After hanging up the phone, I dashed off to the hospital.

Beating the ambulance, I waited outside until the one transporting Tami arrived. The ambulance backed up and stopped, and two paramedics bolted out the rear twin doors, hurriedly pulling out the gurney holding her strapped-in body. Tami was dazed and incoherent. They wheeled her in, and I followed.

After staying seated in the waiting room for what seemed like forever, I finally got to go back in the emergency trauma unit to be with Tami. To add to the atmosphere of worry and stress, across the room, a team of nurses and doctors was working to save a stabbing victim. Awake but still pretty much nonresponsive, she was finally admitted to a room.

Later that afternoon, my parents brought the kids, and they were happy and relieved to see their mom. Even though she was still not doing well, Tami put on her best face for the kids to put them at ease.

James, taking a moment, shared with all of us what Martha had told him: "Living behind that intersection, we had heard many wrecks but never one as loud as Tami's."

Growing tired, Tami kissed all of us goodbye, and I took the kids home.

The next afternoon, Tami was released from the hospital, and I gingerly helped her get into the car and very carefully drove her home.

— 16 —

Tami was now home. The left side of her body was so beat up. To walk, she had to hold on to and lean against my right arm and shoulder, and she was to have complete bed rest. The next day, wanting to spend some time with her, I went home early.

Walking into our bedroom, I said, "Hi baby! How are you doing?"

Still in tremendous pain, she whispered out, "I hear bugs farting in the backyard."

Smiling at her descriptive metaphor, I paused for a moment to process. Taking her reply as a cue, I surmised that her head trauma had also heightened her hearing sensitivity.

After a few days had passed, one evening, I helped her into the bathtub. While keeping a close eye on her, I started looking for the title to our van. Unable to find it, I went into the bathroom and tenderly asked, "Tami, do you know where you put the title to the van?"

After taking a moment, she softy replied, "I don't remember."

I walked back to her dresser and searched a while longer, but to no avail. I asked again, "Tami, I know the insurance company is going to total the van. Are you sure you can't remember where you put the title?"

With the innocence of a young child, confused and frustrated, she said, "Nooo, I can't remember."

Frustrated, I retorted, "You don't know jack crap." I waited in silence for a moment.

Grasping for an answer, she softly replied, "Well…tell me a little bit more about him to see if I can remember."

Frozen and scared, I walked into the bathroom. Seeing her for the first time confused and perplexed, I softly quizzed the airport codes we learned together long ago: "What is SFO [San Francisco airport code]?"

Softly she answered, "I don't know."

Softening my voice, I asked, "Tami, what is LAX [Los Angeles airport code]?"

Again, Tami softly answered, "I don't know."

Wanting to confirm my fear, I asked one more question: "Tami, what is LAS [Las Vegas airport code]?"

Scared and helpless with her memory, sadly and softly, in a lost, defeated voice, Tami replied, "I don't know."

I helped her out of the tub. I dried her off and helped her get dressed. I summoned the kids, and I told them I was taking Mom back to the hospital.

After a few days, the doctors confirmed she had sustained a significant amount of brain trauma.

Back home, Tami continued her bed rest. While I was at work, the LDS church's relief society helped shuttled the kids to and from school, which was a tremendous help to both the kids and me.

Missing her parents, Tami asked one of our kids to dial their number. Imara answered, and Tami asked them to come down.

They arrived the next day. Bob and Imara were a tremendous help to Tami and gave me peace of mind, knowing someone was there to watch over and take care of her.

Imara sat on the edge of our bed. Her heart hurt seeing her daughter in so much pain. She compassionately and patiently prayed that her daughter would recover.

Awake, Tami recognized her mom with a smile and was happy to see her. After talking for a while, Tami was still confused and trying to understand everything. The first question she asked was "Mom, is Gary really my husband?" Imara—the loving, tender, and wise woman that she was—got up and retrieved our wedding album from the living room. As if reading a story to a young child, Imara turned each page of our album and told our story, providing her daughter intricate and intimate details of our wedding and honeymoon.

Peter, our lone opportunist, after I left for work, would come into our bedroom before departing for school and kindly and smoothly proclaim, "Tami, you owe me twenty dollars."

Being the consummate, loving mother, Tami would ask, "I do?"

Peter would then reach for her purse and say, "I'll get it for you, Tami!"

After a few days of Peter getting paid for a fictitious debt, Tami commented to me, "Boy, I sure owe Peter a lot of money!"

Bewildered but more suspicious, I kindly asked, "Tami, can you explain a little bit more?"

In her sweet and innocent voice, she said, "Peter comes in every morning and tells me I owe him twenty-dollars, and then he gets it out of my purse!"

Holding back the disappointed look on my face, I nodded my head. "Baby, let's just consider your debt paid in full."

After leaving our bedroom, I went to have a stern talk with Peter and also retrieve Tami's money.

Of course, I had my moments. As the Super Bowl was approaching, Tami innocently and coincidentally asked, "What do I like?"

I admit it was wrong. But being a "man pig," I confirmed, "You like sex, the color pink, and football!"

I helping her into the living room to watch TV. After the Super Bowl had been on for a while, bored and bewildered, Tami turned her head and asked, "I like this?"

Busted, I confessed, "No, but I thought you could try. I am just glad you are up and we are sitting together."

A little while later, as we were watching one of the Super Bowl commercials, a boy was sucking so hard on a soft drink that he suddenly sucked himself into the bottle. Tami, startled, believing everything she saw was real, exclaimed, "Can that really happen?"

Realizing how upset this had made her, I turned off the game and walked her back to our bedroom, then we lay down together.

Throughout providing care for my wife, I had learned many humbling lessons by helping the woman that I loved and cared for so much.

After Tami had recovered for a few months, I surprised Tami by taking her back to San Diego, and we stayed at the same hotel where we had honeymooned. We went easy on how much walking Tami could do. She did the best she could as we tightly held on to each other while we revisited some of the places in our memories.

Through all of Tami's pain and injury, there was only one thing that I was grateful for in her sustaining a brain injury: the hauntings and memory of her *predator* were gone.

Still having the innocence of a child, she at times had no filter. The first time she met her sisters, she brazenly confessed in front of them while directly speaking to her mom, exclaiming, "They're old!"

There were the tender times, and I thank God I was there to witness them. Shopping together one afternoon, we went to an in-store ATM machine. After entering my password and going through the screen menu, I selected an amount of money. Mesmerized at the inner workings of technology, Tami watched in wonderment as the machine spat out the money.

Noticing that the number keys had raised Braille dots on them, she asked, "Why are there dots on the number keys?"

Smartly, I replied, "That's for blind people!"

Nodding her head, grasping the reasoning, "Oh…okay!"

Walking through the store, Tami quieter than normal, suddenly stopping, turned to me confused, questioned, "How do the blind people see the screen?"

Never ever correlating the two processes needed in operating the machine, I was dumbfounded. Shaking my head, I asked, "Tami, that is an excellent question, and I don't have an answer for you."

One afternoon, while I was outside, working in the front yard, a spring rain had just passed, and I noticed a double rainbow. I quickly grabbed Tami, and we both enjoyed the very special and tender moment.

In the early fall, Las Vegas is treated to some of the biggest moonrises I have ever seen. I walked Tami out to see, and I stood next to her with tears in my eyes as I witnessed her seeing for the first time a full moon. Seeing her eyes filled with such excitement and wonder from witnessing such a never-before-seen magnificent sight for the first time was truly a wondrous moment for both her and me.

The following spring, after much hype and anticipation, we as a family were going back to Disneyland. As we were arriving, Tami was determined and emphatically asked for us not to rent a wheelchair as she was going to walk.

After passing the ticket entrance area, we stood before the Main Street train station. Tami, standing in awe, watched the majestic Disneyland train approach its destination, chugging, clanking, and hissing. With a quick whistle and the crisp train bell ringing out in cheer, it slowly came to a stop. Suddenly a conductor's booming voice announced, "Main Street Station!" as a sea of colorful passengers disembarked.

I held on to Tami, and the kids scattered off, seeking out their own adventures.

We walked up and paused at the railroad bridge, where I showed her Walt Disney's landmark plaque.

HERE YOU LEAVE TODAY
AND ENTER THE WORLD
OF YESTERDAY, TOMORROW,
AND FANTASY

We slowly walked down Main Street, and the sounds from a band playing nearby filled the air as the scents from the candy, ice cream, and other food wafted about us—a teasing ambience.

Passing through Main Street, I noticed Tami was shifting more of her weight onto me. Not saying anything, I slowed down as I pointed out the many hidden details and facts of Disneyland.

Passing in front of the Matterhorn Bobsled's entrance, Tami saw the park benches. Exhausted, in a whispered breath, she asked, "Sweetheart, can we stop for a moment to rest?"

Tenderly and compassionately I said, "Yes, my love."

We were seated, and I held her as she leaned on me for comfort.

After resting a while carefully I finally spoke, "Tami, do you want me to go get a wheelchair?"

Tenderly surrendering, she said, "I tried, honey. I really tried."

I smiled and kissed her forehead. "I know you did, my love. I will be right back!"

I briskly walked back down to the entrance, rented a wheelchair, and quickly returned. A smile quickly overcame my face as I turned the corner and saw Tami now lying down on the park bench.

The area was strangely void of visitors as the Matterhorn had not opened up yet. Setting the brake on the wheelchair, I encouraged, "Here you go, baby!"

Tami raised herself up to sit and exclaimed, "I saw Mickey and Minnie!"

I was smiling but confused. "I didn't know they had come up this far yet."

She giggled. "No, not the characters! There are two mice in the flower bed!"

We laughed in unison, and I helped her into the wheelchair. We both together—and with our kids—helped her rediscover the magic kingdom of Disneyland!

$$\sim 17 \sim$$

As each week passed, Tami continued to slowly improve. She was still childlike, and her clairvoyance was beyond imagination. Here are a few small samples (even though there were many more).

She was trying to learn my direct back-line work phone number. The number had been the same since I had started with the company.

When I came home, she greeted me by bursting out, "I found a way to remember your work phone number!"

Excited and curious, I asked, "That is great, my love! How did you do it?"

"By looking at the alphabet shown below, on the phone keys! The last four digits of the phone number spells Gary!"

I shook my head in amazement. "Baby, it's so amazing how you did that! After working so long with that number and being such an integral part of our department, I could have never imagined my name correlated with the last four digits."

A few weeks later, Tami was standing in front of my office door, which read Service Manager.

Reading the words slowly, she deciphered loudly, "Service Man Ager."

I shot a shocked look at her as I shook my head. "You are so right. Not many people understand or, for that fact, care what a stressful job this really is. This job really is a man ager."

Wanting to be more helpful to her family, one morning, alone, Tami decided to pull the weeds in our front flower bed. As she was still very weak and working for an unknown time, the heat was finally getting to her. Just about to pass out, she just managed to call me with our wireless phone, which, luckily, she had with her. With her voice weak and garbled, I was able to decipher that she was working outside and in trouble. It took me only ten minutes to get home. I found her lying down, incoherent, and disorientated. After getting her to her feet, I helped her into the house and laid her down on our bed. I wetted some towels with cold water, and using them, I was able to cool her down and revive her.

Smiling, I tenderly spoke, "Baby, you need to be careful in the heat. You don't need to be working outside. You still need to be resting and getting better."

Frustrated, she said, "You and the kids do so much for me. I get so tired of being a burden to you all."

I sat down on the bed, hugged her, and very tenderly spoke, "I understand how you feel. But there are also five of us that love you very much. We want you to get better so you can again do things around the house that you loved doing. But this will happen in due time when you get better, and we don't care how long it takes because we love you and care for you more than anything else."

After the accident, one thing that both Tami and I wanted to do was for me to take Temple classes so we could both go to the Temple together.

Holding the classes at a private residence, both the husband and wife were very kind and personable. The husband possessed a tremendous amount of knowledge and did a wonderful job teaching.

One night, somehow, he got off the subject and started telling one of his childhood stories about him and his father working in their ranch in Wyoming.

He was a gentle-looking man, and I always sensed that if he had to, he could hold his own. He started his story.

"My dad was an honest man, but he could also be a hard man. While working our herd, we came upon one of our calves that had been killed by a predator. My dad was concerned but not mad. He asked me to get off my horse. Together we lifted the calf, and my dad securely tied the calf onto my horse. I was riding with my dad as we headed back to the ranch, and my dad commented on why removing the calf had to be done, explaining to me that if we did nothing, it would be like ringing a dinner bell and inviting even more predators.

"A few weeks went by, and just our luck, we saw the dog from a nearby ranch viciously chasing our calves. My dad quickly grabbed his rifle and fired off a few warning shots. The dog quickly ran back home. Following the dog, we approached the house as the neighbor came out to greet us.

"My dad was a kind and cordial man, but when he got mad, his mannerism was curt and right to the point. He told the neighbor about what he had just witnessed and of his prior loss. My dad pointed his finger at the neighbor and in a deep, not-to-be-misunderstood voice, promised, 'If I catch that dog bothering my herd again, I will shoot him dead.'

"My dad stared at the neighbor for a moment before yanking the reins on his horse as he stabbed his heels into the horse's sides. He called out for me to follow as he galloped away.

"Several weeks later, we again came upon the dog again bothering our herd. The dog, on seeing us, got scared and bolted into a run as he headed home again. My dad, angry, rode fast and hard. I just managed to keep up.

"We were galloping up to the neighbor's house. The panting dog, nervous, paced in front of his master, who was standing on the porch steps.

"My dad came to a sudden stop. The horse's hooves dug into the soft dirt. My dad sternly spoke, 'Mike, I told you I would shoot that dog if I caught him bothering my herd again.'

"The neighbor stammered, looking for an answer, but was not as quick as my father. My dad drew out his rifle, and he *shot the dog dead*."

Suddenly Tami began shaking as if she were having a seizure. Unable to speak, I held on to her tightly as I knew what had just happened.

The instructor, confused and feeling bad and upset, stood up. I helped Tami to the door as I answered, "It's okay. I just need to take her home."

Years earlier, Tami was confronted with the horror from the sudden loss of her dog. Seeing her dog shot, she was devastated as her father stood by silently as the *predator* spoke, "Bob, this dog was chasing my horses, so *I shot the dog dead.*"

The *predator*, who had been held at bay for only a short time from her memory, once again returned to haunt Tami's life.

It was the memory of her dead dog, who was purposely killed to reinforce, control, and silence Tami.

The *predator*, once again haunting, ghostly whispered, *"You tell anyone, and I will kill you and your family."*

~⟶ **18** ⟵~

Never quite back to 100 percent, Tami had recovered over time as the four kids one by one became teenagers. Each in their own time turned to Mom in their times of need.

The two older kids—Catherine and James—double dated, and their dates soon grew into deeply involved first loves. Over time, as with most first loves, subsequently, Catherine and James suffered from traumatic and very emotional breakups roughly six months apart.

Catherine took her breakup hard. Not only had she lost her boyfriend, but also, the breakup rekindled and triggered the long-ago emotions from the loss of her dad, which compounded her pain.

Tami spent motherly healing time with her, and she allowed Catherine to miss as much school as she needed as they both worked on repairing and reviving her broken soul.

With James's breakup, she stayed close to James and provided her love and support. She would sleep on the floor next to his bed, and she also let him miss a few days of school as she helped James work out the pain of losing his first love and disappointment.

No matter which one of her four children needed help, Mom was there to help no matter what they needed her to do or what she could do to make life a little more understandable and bearable.

Tami commented to me many times, "If anyone messes with my kids, the sweet, lovable disposition can and will turn into a very formidable tiger."

Peter, different, was one of the easiest kids to raise. As he was never around much, we deemed him our official teenage "secret agent."

Embellishing a typical conversation with Peter, she used to joke over a typical jousting conversation, "Peter, where are you going?"

Peter would reply calmly, "Mom, wherever you need me to go or whatever you need me to do or pick up for you, I will go there and do it."

Through all the verbal wordplay, Peter came and went unfettered and, most importantly, always undercover!

Sunday was the only day in all the kids' work schedules where we could all sit down for dinner together. Since we were living in Las Vegas, our dinner discussions with the kids were open and frank. Tami and I wanted to prepare our kids the best we could for the unexpected that the culture of Las Vegas served up.

I think the scariest things we found out came later in life as parents, and it was when we sat down with our kids and finally found out the truth of what really happened while they were together with their friends.

Mary, the baby, gave us the most problems, and yes, blame it all on my genes. My mother's mother and my mother always said in a cautionary tone when talking about dealing with the ups and downs of life, "You pay for your raising," and boy did I ever.

One morning in particular, Tami was driving Mary and one of her friends. Mary, in full throttle, was giving her a hard time. As things reached a crescendo, Mary played a card she had never played before, knowing it would hurt her mom the most. She made a crass comment about her weight.

Hurt and having had quite enough, Tami retorted in a sarcastic tone, "Well, at least I am not a bony whore."

Mary's friend, although shocked, burst out in hysterical laughter at Tami's unfettered quick comeback. Many years later, Mary's friend would remind and tease Tami and Mary of the awkward but cherished memory as now all three could laugh about it.

We bought a spa to help Tami recover from her accident, and one evening, we noticed the fiberglass filter cover was cracked. We wondered what happened, and years later Catherine told us it broke during one of her and James's parties as they wanted to see how many people could fit into our spa.

One weekend, Tami and I took her oldest sister's kids to Disneyland. As we were getting ready to return home, we received a call from Peter. Very calm, Peter began, "Hey, I know you guys are heading home today, but I wanted to give you guys a heads-up. We had some friends over last night, and things got out of sorts, and a kid ran into Josh with his car as he was leaving. But he is okay. I just wanted to let you know everything is fine."

We handed the phone back and forth between us, but as much as we asked, nothing more or less changed in Peter's details. We quickly headed home.

As we arrived home, the story quickly gelled into hard facts. Mary and her friend were at a guy's house. The guy was pressuring them for sex while he was high, but Mary and her friend said no and quickly talked him into going to her brother's party. After arriving at our house, Mary talked to Peter, and her friend talked to her brother Jake, who was also one of Peter's best friends. After they told Peter and Jake how much of a jerk this guy was, they asked him to leave. A scuffle quickly broke out, and Peter and Jake together physically escorted him to his car. The boy, right after getting into his car, gunned it to the end of our cul-de-sac, quickly turning around, and swerved at the last minute, hitting Jake and running over his leg.

Someone called the cops and paramedics, and while they were waiting, the party quickly dispersed. The paramedics arrived and took Jake to the hospital where he stayed in for a few weeks. Sadly, to this day, Jake still suffers pain. Later that night, the police arrested the boy for committing a hit-and-run and leaving the scene of an accident, and he was eventually convicted.

As we were standing outside, in front of our house, one of our neighbors came up to talk to Tami and me. Coincidentally, the neighbor's wife was studying to be a crime scene investigator. But after helping spray the blood off the street and into the gutter drain, he told us that after the horror of what happened the previous night, she was changing her career choice.

With four teenagers and us living in Vegas, I told Tami we had better odds of getting hit by an asteroid than we did having our marriage surviving as a teenage blended family.

We dodged the asteroid, and both our marriage and our kids survived. In the end, we always felt we deserved very little credit for having all four of our kids turn out as well as they did. Because in the end, the reality was that it was always up to them.

⁓ 19 ⁓

Wanting to get away from work and needing to take a vacation, I arranged for us to take a trip to San Diego. As an added surprise, my old friend Mike, who lived in San Diego, invited us to go sailing on his boat. We were always observing the sailboats from Point Loma Lighthouse, and this would be the first time for both of us to actually sail on one.

After we boarded the boat, Mike went over some quick safety and sailing instructions.

Casting off, we left the marina as we motored out to the inlet of San Diego Harbor.

Tami and I, following Mike's patient instructions, together hoisted the sails as Mike's eyes were keenly focused on the wind indicator on top of the mast. As he turned the wheel, the sails, suddenly catching the wind, snapped, and they gently started pulling us forward.

Mike reached down and shut off the engine. We both realized for the first time in our lives the sound of *silence* as we headed out under God's power into the vast Pacific Ocean.

Both Tami and I were in awe, then my mind flashed to the scene from the movie *Titanic* where the confident Captain Edward Smith, in charge of this huge vessel, in a proud, gentlemanly tone said to the first officer, "Take her to sea, Mr. Murdoch. Let's stretch her legs!"

We were having such a great time that Mike invited us out a few years later to sail again. We sailed out and spent the night moored off the Mexican-held Coronado Island.

Sailing in a stiff, constant breeze, we watched Tami at the bow of the boat as it sliced and parted the Pacific Ocean. As we splashed high along the sides, the salty ocean spray filled our senses.

Mike and I gleefully enjoyed watching Tami, especially when a pod of dolphins joined us as they raced and jumped along the side of the bow of the boat. Tami was excited. After challenging us in both speed and splash, the dolphins easily won.

We wanted to sail more; and another dear friend, David, offered to teach me how to sail on the weekends as a member of his crew as we competed with other racing sailboats on Lake Mead. Learning a lot, both Tami and I agreed that with Mike and David having so many years of sailing experience, we should have no fears in putting our lives in their hands. They were both confident and very skilled heavy-weather sailors.

Both of us were reaching a different point in life with our kids. Catherine was in her own apartment and attending college. James was enlisted in the Navy. Peter, now graduated, spent most of his time with his friend's family, and when he wasn't with them, he was with us or making sure Mary stayed out of trouble. Mary was still at home as a sophomore in high school. We were almost empty-nesters.

Taking a few days off in late spring, Tami and I traveled to Lake Mead and visited all the marinas, hoping and dreaming of one day owning a sailboat.

As we looked at the sailboats, an old saying kept creeping into my mind: "I prefer my dream to stay a dream. The payments are cheaper!"

A few weeks later, on returning home, Tami met me at the door, took my hand, and led me to the dining room table. I was a bit confused. She had everything set out and in order. Excited, she presented me the loan documents and exclaimed, "Gary, we can do this! You can have your dream of owning a sailboat!"

Happy that she loved me so much to have done this for me, I grabbed her, and we hugged and kissed for the longest time. I was truly a blessed and a lucky man to have such a loving wife.

I asked David to help us find a good boat, and he soon called and told me he found our sailboat.

We went to the Marina, looked at the boat, and got the contact information. We then arranged a meeting with the owner, and he showed us the boat and took us out for a short sail. Satisfied, we shook hands on a tentative deal. We and the owner met a few days later, and we were now proud owners of a sailboat.

Settling on a name was easy for me. Being a *Titanic* buff, I wanted to have some semblance to the name Titanic.

With our family all present, Tami christened her *Titamic*, which reflected four hidden messages:

(1) My love for the *Titanic.*
(2) My love for Tami (Ti*tamic*).
(3) Not tempting the gods as this boat *was* sinkable!
(4) With Tami being large breasted, the first three letters addressed that attribute!

Working the next two weekends, we transformed *Titamic* in to our sacred and private retreat to escape and just relax and concentrate on each other.

Our typical weekend on the boat consisted of fixing Friday-night dinners. Tami would be in the galley, fixing a salad and setting the table, while I was on the bow, grilling our steaks and baked potatoes.

Finished with dinner, we would play Backgammon. She held her own, and if you looked at the games where one lost and the other won, you'd see that each game was almost always a virtual tie.

Throughout our marriage, Tami loved to play board and card games, with Backgammon being our favorite. Most importantly, the best feature the boat brought out in us was that we both talked and listened!

As it got late, we would venture down to the marina showers for an always-interesting shower experience. The room, no more than five feet by ten feet, consisted of a shower and a vanity sink and made anything more than just standing a chore. As a prelude to a romantic evening on the boat, our intimacy started in the small shower stall while we contorted our bodies and took turns soaping and rinsing each other off. Then we'd return to the boat. On pleasant nights, we would sit out under the stars as I held Tami in my arms and lose ourselves in the moment.

Retiring belowdecks, Tami would pull out the bed and make it while I secured the hatch and turned on soft music, thus setting the mood.

On windy nights, the lanyard lines tapping against the steel mast mimicked a unique peaceful wind chime. The boat would sway softly back and forth, gently tugging on its mooring lines, while we made love and peacefully fell asleep in each other's arms.

After getting up on Saturday morning, I'd cast off the mooring lines and jump on the boat as Tami, at the helm, backed us out. Leaving the dock, Captain Tami navigated us out of the harbor as I hoisted and adjusted the sails. Then she'd cut the power to the engine.

Sailing around the lake for the next four hours, we were often alone. Taking advantage of that, Tami wanted to work on her tan. Again, she was not bashful and would pull the top part of her one-piece bathing suit down.

Sailing, quiet, free, and at peace, we worked together and loved being with each other as best friends, lovers, and soulmates.

After calling it a day, Tami would motor us back to the marina while I lowered, secured, and covered the sails. As we pulled up to our berth, even with an unpredictable wind, Tami would always skillfully bring *Titamic* in, and I would jump on the dock to steady the boat and secure it with the mooring lines.

Heading back to Vegas was always the saddest time for both of us. For me, every mile we got closer to Vegas, the more the pressure of work increased as I mentally prepared for another week. For my baby, it was losing our special alone time as we merged back with our Monday-through-Friday routine.

~ **20** ~

In the spring of 2001, we celebrated our tenth anniversary. Working under tremendous daily stress, I was having neurological problems, and the medical prognosis for a long life was soon diagnosed. It was not good.

For the first time in Tami's life, she was confident and happy with herself, her looks, and her weight. This news rattled her to the point of a panic attack. Throughout her life, she endured many things. However, enduring the hauntings of her past and going through another loss and being left alone was, for her, sheer terror.

To help us stay engaged with each other and have a distraction of hope, we immersed ourselves in our passion and joined the local yacht club. We learned new sailing skills, and as a bonus, we also met new friends as we shared the same degree of passion with many of the members.

Our weekends now consisted of racing, night sailing races, sailing classes, and a few restaurant meetings in Las Vegas.

For Tami, this was something new and adventurous as this was the first time in her life where she had associated friendship attached to the love of a sport. As always, she was the life of the events and parties, with always a surprise or two to entertain, and she'd laugh with our friends at her own antics.

One weekend, I was treated with great pride as I watched her and her crew race in the Women's Regatta, and to my concerned amusement, she got our boat stuck on a shallow shoal. Working quickly, Tami started the motor and put it into reverse power. *Titamic* was quickly set free, and they were able to finish the race. Even though they didn't win a ribbon, she enjoyed sailing with her crew; and ribbon or not, they finished with tremendous pride and a sense of accomplishment.

Back at work, after going through a few secretaries, I hired Tami as my secretary. The beautiful part about working for the company I worked for, since it was a family-owned company, was that the word *nepotism* was never any part or a question of concern. Also, as an unspoken benefit, I joked with Tami that she could not accuse me of sexual harassment!

Excited, she finally got to see my world, and soon the names we talked about for so long had faces.

A quick learner, she soon became very proficient in doing her job and loved doing it. She was a little worried about how the crew would accept her, but they quickly grew to love her positive and bubbly personality and every once in a while shared a good laugh.

With Tami's parents' anniversary coming up, she asked if she could fly up and be with them for the weekend. I agreed, dropped off her at the airport on Friday morning, and went to work.

As I sat at my desk, the phone rang. As I picked it up, I immediately heard Tami in a cheerful voice asking, "Do you miss me yet!"

I laughed and replied, "Why, as a matter of fact, yes, I do!"

She laughed, then quickly asked, "Hey, would you mind if I buy my parents a new kitchen sink as our anniversary present to them?"

"If that is what they want, I think it would be a great present for them. Tell them I said hello and wish them a happy anniversary for me. I love you!"

Tami, gleeful, said, "I will and thank you!"

I did not hear much from Tami over the weekend, and I picked her up at the airport.

On the drive home, still excited about seeing her parents and family, she filled me in on all the news.

Curious about our present, I asked, "So how did you parents like the kitchen sink?"

"They liked it a lot and needed one very badly."

Engaged in driving but curious, I queried, "Who installed it for them?"

She answered quickly, "I called Dave, and since he does not have a job right now, he put it in for them."

Nodding my head, I asked, "How much did he charge you?"

Tami, upbeat, responded, "Nothing! He just wanted to help me out."

Many months later, Tami confessed that after the sink was installed, later on in the late evening, she drove her parents' car to a nearby elementary school and met Dave.

To my disheartened shock, she told me passion and emotions went too far and that she had surrendered herself to him.

Faced with a Nancy problem that presented itself once again, I asked the questions that needed to be asked. Satisfied with Tami's remorse and honesty and learning from my mistake from the past, I forgave her.

Many years later, as part of the final puzzle completed, Tami told me a few weeks after they had been together that Dave's wife had called to tell her that she and Dave were getting divorced because of their actions.

As time passed, the stress of my mental health started to weigh in, and it also affected Tami. Still working with me, she and my assistant helped share some of my workload.

It wasn't until months later that Tami went to our bishop, and with the convening of a bishop's court to relieve her guilty conscience, Tami confessed her past. Before leaving, she asked the court not to tell me about what she had confessed in her involvement with my assistant, which they honored.

A few days later, Tami confessed to me what they had done.

While I was in the Los Angeles area for the weekend, all their previous actions had eventually culminated into a Saturday-night rendezvous. Tami told her parents (who were visiting with us at the time) that she was going swimming at her best friend's house. She met her best friend at a casino, and she confessed it was all a ruse, them spending any time together. Tami instead told her friend of her plans for the night and for her to provide cover for her if her parents called. Tami called my assistant, and he told Tami something had come up and that the night was called off. Tami, completing her confession, ended by telling me nothing happened and that she went back home and watched *The Tonight Show* with her mom.

The hurtful betrayal of an affair is crushing. A couple engaged in an affair means that for one or the other, or both, either love comes into play, or it is just sex. An affair, by default, comes with all the human emotions, which, by definition, means there is a precipice of choice between what you have and some deficiency in what you are missing in your marriage or relationship.

Having lived in Las Vegas, I can say that what happens in Las Vegas does not stay in Las Vegas as the stories that affect you personally always stays with you.

Allow me to segue. My mother was friends with a married prostitute, and they would visit and go to lunch from time to time. One day, I asked my mom out of curiosity, "Mom, how does her husband stay with her, knowing what she does with other men?"

My mother drew a deep breath and said, "I have asked her that very question. She told me that her husband loves her very much, and she loves him very much. And they cannot live one without the other. Crazy as it seems, I guess that somehow, for them…it just works out."

Listening to Tami finish explaining what happened that night, my love and trust were tested as I knew she was not telling the truth. *The Tonight Show* was only broadcasted on weekdays, not on Saturdays.

I wanted to believe her because I believed *in* her. Never challenging her on this factual error, I let it pass as I was coming to the realization that Tami and I deeply loved each other. Love is a testament to a commitment that knows no boundaries.

The ruling of the bishop's court was for Tami to be disfellowshipped.

Our bishop, who was also a counselor, wanted to help Tami, so he told her in private that she had all the characteristics of a sexual addict and advised her to seek out some professional help, which both hurt and infuriated her.

After she returned home from church, I remember Tami was sad and remorseful as the church she was born into and loved so much; through her actions, it had all led to this.

It would be some time before Tami returned to church. The hangover from sexual addiction is parallel to a recovering drunk alcoholic calling out to the bartender, "Make it a double."

❧ 21 ☙

As time progressed, my health was getting more unmanageable until it finally reached a point where I could no longer put in the hours or handle the stress of trying to keep up with the demands of a twenty-four-hour job servicing the casino industry.

I retired, and we sold our house and, sadly, our sailboat. Many years later, we were missing our intimate togetherness time on the sailboat. Lamenting, Tami would always tell me she wished we had never moved to Utah and just kept the sailboat and lived on it.

We quickly bought a house in Roy, Utah, and within a few weeks, Tami got a job. Staying home, I became the househusband.

When she came home each night, I would enjoy listening to her tell me about her day at work.

Part of her job was to work with an outside contractor. Keeping me in the dark, she soon became involved with a man; and together they ran the gamut from friends to good friends, which quickly culminated as sexual relations.

What was once consensual quickly turned into him controlling her, which included stalking and ended with him forcefully entering our house and raping her.

Out of town, I soon received a call from her mom and returned the next day as Tami was in the hospital for psychiatric observation from being raped.

I took her home, terrified. For the next few days, Tami confessed her guilt and involvement. She also told me that this man, while once involved in law enforcement, had shot and killed a man with a shotgun while he was running away from him. He also had a talent of being able to pick locks.

I made sure Tami took her prescriptions; they greatly helped her calm down as I tucked her into bed and let her get as much rest and sleep as she needed. For the next three days, I stayed awake both day and night, armed and by her side, and I took quick catnaps when she was awake.

Again, Tami was dealing with a predator, and this time it was self-induced as she had ignored all the warning signs.

Dealing with hang-up phone calls from phone booths, Tami was angry and wanted this to stop. Tami and I agreed, and we went to the proper authorities and filled out the stalking-injunction paperwork.

Hating this man for what he had done and the pain he inflicted, I wanted to turn the tables from being the hunted to being the hunter.

Looking for weaknesses, I did very extensive forensic research, and it didn't take long to figure out he cherished his guns. Having filled out the stalking-injunction paperwork, we subsequently went to court. If the injunction was enforced, he would lose his guns.

On the day of the court hearing, we were working with the state's attorneys through negotiation between both parties, and an agreement was reached. We would withdraw the injunction on a certain agreement, and the agreement was predicated on the condition that he would never have any contact with or harass us. If he violated the terms of the agreement, the stalking injunction would immediately be reinstated. Also having the injunction on file would also serve as a strong deterrent if he wanted to kill or harm us as he would be the first and most likely suspect of an investigation.

For the next six months, with me having a conceal-carry permit and being armed, every day I took and picked up Tami from work and any other public place she wanted or needed to go to.

Throughout all of our marriage, whenever Tami was down, she always wanted a dog close by. I got her a puppy, and this helped her immensely in comforting her battered soul.

One night returning home, walking into our bedroom, the puppy's toys were mysteriously lined up, looking as if it was a highway center dividing line as it led into our bedroom. Tami was freaking out, so I held her tightly, assuring her that no one had been in our house. I settled her down, but I never told her my true suspicions and the high probability that he could have been in our house. As a precaution, for the next week, I again resumed my routine of keeping an around-the-clock watch over Tami.

As time passed, I knew it would be a big risk for this man to resume his activities in bothering Tami. I also drew comfort in one thing. This predator was now in his late sixties, and I knew a leopard's spots never change but do, however, fade away with age.

In my later years, I often thought about this man's predatory years. Sadly, I somehow knew there were other victims and wondered how many lives were forever damaged and changed.

After a few months, I noticed Tami was gaining an extreme amount of weight. Understanding the cause and effect, this once again reinforced to me her long-standing protective mantra: "I put on weight so no man would want me."

Together, attending a party one evening, Tami's best friend was taking a group picture of a much heavier Tami. Next to her, a man, while holding his drink, unknowingly pressed it into the side of one of her breasts. Many years later, as I looked at the captured image, I finally understood why Tami had such a terrified look on her face.

Shortly thereafter, our daughter Mary and our son-in-law moved in with us. Within ten months, we were blessed with our first grandchild. We helped our daughter adapt as a first-time mommy. This was truly a joyful event for her. Between all four of us, we provided more love than was needed, but for Tami, she could never give her enough love.

Tami, still working in the same department, continued to do well. Knowing her and the industry she was in, it really wasn't a good fit for either one of them.

After a year, to her devastation, the company let her go. That was the first and only time she was ever terminated by an employer.

Tami accepted responsibility for her actions, and as her boss escorted her out of the building, her boss thanked her and was sorry it had ended like this. Reciprocating, Tami thanked her for the opportunity and appreciated both her and all her coworkers for the opportunity to work with them.

With me now working a small part-time job, Tami took time to both heal her battered soul and be a full-time grandma.

Every once in a while, Tami's dear friend Travis would stop to see all of us; or we would stop by to visit Travis and also go to a few of his parties. Helping us move in and also helping me when Tami was raped, he was a good friend to us.

For the longest time after her rape, the only two men Tami could trust that would not hurt her were me and Travis.

With our daughter, our son-in-law, and our granddaughter moving back to Las Vegas, it was truly a sad day. Tami had only been able to give birth to Catherine, and both of us had always wished we could have been able to have a child of our own.

With our first grandchild living with us, we both got to experience that feeling and were very blessed to have her as well as all the future grandkids yet to come.

Part of Grandma's secret to being so much fun was that she was still a kid herself at heart. So while Tami was growing down, the grandchildren were growing up. Thankfully, there was always somewhere in the middle for grandma and the grandchildren to all have some crazy kid time.

We were soon blessed with our second grandchild, and Tami was able to fly to Augusta, Georgia, and spent a week with Peter and his wife, helping and getting to know our newest grandchild. Sadly, distance, time, and money were always a struggle, so visits were rare.

Within a year, Mary was now divorced and returned with Amanda to live with us. Now she was a single mom, and we again were glad to help them in any way we could. With Mary now twenty-four and single, she would go out with a lot with her friends, which gave us some alone time with Amanda.

Mary, again within a year, moved back to Vegas and moved in with my mom. Now we were both free for the first time in a long time. We were truly just husband and wife as all of our kids now lived in different states.

Tami, like her father, went by this code: "Better to ask for forgiveness than permission." This permeated into Tami's thinking and actions.

With Travis and Tami being each other's firsts, she could never say goodbye, and occasionally they would get together.

Maybe months, maybe a year, and sometimes never, Tami would confess to me that she had been with Travis. How could I let this happen? For most men, this would be a nonnegotiable cause for terminating a marriage. For me—and I am sure it was the same for her—there were times of uncertainty. But knowing Tami's past and her indiscretions, I knew she loved me just as much as she had loved Dirk. Most importantly, I loved her like I had never loved another woman. This is why I stayed.

Our marriage worked and survived because I learned the magic word that had eluded me for so long in my life, including during the destruction of my first marriage. The magic word was *forgiveness*.

— 22 —

Eventually Tami went back to work. Tami got a secretarial job at the same mortuary that helped her with Dirk's funeral. The owner once commented, "I had never hired such an overqualified woman to take a secretarial position, but I am glad I did."

Tami was always very kind and compassionate to the ones in mourning. Because she lost Dirk when she was so young, she knew the pain and suffering from the loss of a loved one.

She also brought joy and happiness and was dearly loved by her coworkers. The funeral directors always gave their hearts and souls while working with the families, and Tami could always be counted on to cheer them up with her comedic passion. She helped them feel better during their times they were down.

Oftentimes Tami was sacrilegious to a fault. One afternoon, there was a problem with the settings of the crematory oven. The mishap had never happened before; and the owner, deeply embarrassed by the electronic malfunction, apologized to her for the smoke.

Tami being Tami, she did not show any disrespect or irreverence. Instead, she tried to lighten the moment, dryly commenting, "Next time, less barbeque sauce."

Another afternoon, Tami brought our granddaughter to work. She also brought some toys and books to keep her entertained since Amanda had never been to Grandma's work or a funeral home.

Looking up, Amanda spoke in an affirmative voice, "Grandma, the people downstairs are very happy."

Stunned, she softly questioned, "Amanda, who told you there was a downstairs?"

Amanda, playing with her toy, was sure of herself and said, "No one, Grandma."

Now she was more curious. "Well, how did you know there was a downstairs?"

Amanda, in a trusting, innocent voice, answered, "The people told me."

Approaching the end of the year, since Tami was witnessing so many spiritual encounters and working with such righteous religious coworkers, we went back to church.

As the new year began, with the help and influence of a loving and remarkable ward and its leaders, Tami was rebaptized.

One morning, as she was at her eye appointment, Tami was in her full gala and having fun with the opticians and store manager. Recognizing talent, the manager soon asked if she would like to work at their store. Gleefully accepting, she sadly gave her two weeks' notice to the mortuary.

Throughout our marriage, Tami possessed and exhibited her abilities of being smart, talented, and goal driven. The only Achilles heel that always held her back was not having enough confidence in herself.

Learning a new field, all the medical procedures and terms sometimes stretched her ability to grasp the optical field; and after a few months, with the help of a coworker that would soon turn into a lifelong friend, she was patiently guided and taught all the necessary requirements to be a great optician.

Working well with the patients, she was soon assigned to be the store closer.

Before closing the store at 7:00 PM, Tami would work on insurance and balancing the final drop while I vacuumed the store. When we got home, which was around 8:00 PM, I would fix a late dinner while she relaxed.

One evening, the Ogden police brought in a severely challenged little girl. Born with vision problems, she had only seen her world as fuzzy and blurred.

Retrieving the little girl's glasses, Tami talked to her in her soft voice and tenderly put the thick-lensed glasses on the little girl. What was once viewed as a skewed, fuzzy kaleidoscope of forms suddenly snapped into focus, reveling Tami's happy face. Fighting back her tears, Tami was grateful and so blessed to have witnessed such a monumental event as the little girl smiled at her.

When an opportunity to be a store manager became available, Tami jumped at the chance. She took over an old store, and she was soon able to turn around business enough that the owners negotiated for a new store to be built a few doors up from the old store.

When Tami moving into the new store, sales took off. Part of her success was how she treated her patients and her staff, and she had the amazing ability to remember names.

Also, some people from time to time, as if in a *Field of Dreams* moment ("If you build it, they will come"), would wander in and not know why. Once they sat down, they would open up and tell her their problems.

Full of empathy, love, and care, Tami would listen; and in the end, after making them feel better, she would wish them well and ask them to stop by anytime.

One perk she received when working for the company was the discounts for buying glasses, which were also afforded to me.

Throughout her life, Tami had a hard time accepting compliments. Every once in a while, I would look deeply into her eyes, mine full of emotion and love, and say, "Honey, you are so beautiful."

She would smile, then sympathetically retort, "Baby, we can't afford to keep buying you glasses!"

Soon after moving into her store, we met a husband and wife and soon became close friends. We would go out to dinner and have dinner at each other's houses. It was always a treat, and our friendship meant so much to the four of us.

With Tami, the employee-management part of her job was always a struggle for her. She was feeling good about one individual's interview and subsequent employment, but he was not working out. He called in sick the first day, and all went downhill from there. Tami came home many nights complaining out of frustration to me, and I patiently listened.

After a few nights of empathizing and trying to make her feel better, I finally said, "Tami, you need to fire this person, and if you can't, you need to fire yourself."

Not liking that scenario, she snapped, "I can't do it."

I nodded my head in agreement. "I know. But when you are a manager, you set the tone and the expectations. If you do nothing, in time, you will lose the respect you worked so hard to get from the rest of your staff. Instead of just having one problem employee, your problems will multiply."

She slept on it, and the next morning, as she was driving to work, she still seemed rattled and uncertain about what to do.

I was already at work when I picked up my cell phone, and seeing it was Tami brought a smile to my face. "Good morning, my love!"

She was still heavy with indecision, which reflected in the tone of her voice. "Hello, my love."

Picking up her vibes, I asked, "Hey, I am sorry for what you are going through. Please know one thing. I love you, and I will support you in whatever decision you make."

After ending our call, I took a deep breath and said a silent prayer.

I received a call about two hours later. Tami still sounded upset and said in a rattled voice, "This was one of the hardest things I have ever had to do. But it is done."

The most enduring Christlike quality Tami possessed was that she always helped the poor by giving them money. One such example is a story she shared with me. As part of her work routine, she liked to arrive early to work each morning. One morning, on the way to work, she picked up breakfast to go. While eating her breakfast behind the front counter, she noticed a homeless man going through the trash can in front of the store. Tami looked down at her half-eaten meal. She then picked it up and hurried to the front door. She unlocking the door and held out the enclosed Styrofoam container. "Hi. I'm Tami. I stopped and picked this up, but I just can't finish it. Please take it."

The man, straightening up, took a moment to look at Tami. Expressionless, he calmly turned as he stuffed the rummaged trash back into the container and slowly walked away.

For the next few days, she again watched the man go through the trash can. Not done, she came up with another plan. The next morning, she again picked up breakfast. Approaching the store, Tami stopped and stuffed it into the trash.

Tami saw the man approach. Filled with hope, she watched him dig through the trash. He picked up the white Styrofoam container and slowly opened it. He reaching in. The man began eating with his hands as he slowly walked away.

> The truth about it is, whether we is rich or poor or somethin in between, this earth ain't no final restin place. So in a way, we is all homeless—just working our way toward home. (Denver Moore)

Widowed so young in life and shattered into grief from the loss of Dirk, Tami briefly attended some classes on grief.

She was invited over one afternoon by a long grieving widow for a visit, and the woman asked if she would accompany her down to the basement bedrooms. Following, she was led to one particular bedroom.

The widow turned and said, "This is where I put my husband's things. I come down here, and this is where I grieve. It is quiet down here, and no one can hear me. This is where I find myself free to let go and release my pain and sorrow."

Just then, the woman broke out into a guttural scream that seemed to have no end. Now quiet, the woman was sitting down on the bed, sad and lonely. Her tears, knowing the path down to the end of her cheeks, dropped uncounted.

Grief knows no bounds and has been with humankind since the beginning of time. The Egyptians, knowing the loss of sorrowed grief, would collect their tears in a small decorated vial. So precious was the loss that the vial would be left with their loved ones for their afterlife as a tribute to the love that once was.

Feeling very sorry and helpless, Tami tried the best she could to comfort and help the long-surviving widow.

Driving home, she thought, *There has got to be a better way to help people in their grief.*

In her experience, funerals were short-lived, and the life of grief was always unpredictable.

Tami shared a story of an event that happened just after losing Dirk. She confessed, "People most of the time don't know what to say or do when they see you and somehow become frozen. One day, I was grocery shopping and saw a friend start to come down the same aisle I was shopping in. Seeing me, she was startled, turned around, and went to another aisle to avoid talking to me."

One morning, at the optical store, she received a call from the grief facilitator of the mortuary. Excited to hear from her, she soon let Tami know that she was leaving her position and wondered if she would be interested in taking over her grief classes. Excited, Tami jumped at the chance. Tami said yes. After she met with the owner, he immediately agreed to having her represent them in facilitating their grief classes.

So happy in helping the grieving, she would later confess, "Being an optical manager pays the bills. Being a grief facilitator pays a grateful heart." As a caveat, she also would tell others, "In one job, I help people see. In my other job, I help people see themselves through their grief and learn to live again."

— 23 —

Throughout her adult life, Tami always had trouble with her neck. When we were dating, every so often, she would suddenly and loudly snap her neck to the left and then to the right.

Her father often commented on it, giving a cautious warning to her of the trouble she would have with her neck as she got older.

On reaching that point in her life, she finally went to see a specialist and was diagnosed that she needed to have neck surgery. She had plates and screws installed on both sides of her neck. It was a rough surgery.

I took her home to rest; and later that afternoon, she suddenly sat up in bed, startled. "I have a grief class tonight!"

Sitting by her, I calmly said, "Tami, you are in no shape to go tonight. You need to rest."

Determined and possessed, she insisted, "I have to go. There are so many people coming, and this is the first class in the series."

Understanding and not questioning, I helped get her ready and drove her to the library where all the sessions were held.

I seated Tami, and as all the grieving participants came in, she warmly greeted them in her cheerful and hopeful voice in spite of her being in tremendous masked pain.

She did not fool the grieving participants that night and gained tremendous respect and admiration for her passion and dedication in wanting to help them.

Always accompanying her to the sessions, I got to witness the progression of each one of the grievers as I watched Tami piece by piece help them with their shattered, perplexed, and emotional puzzle. The puzzles would end up somewhat complete, and the only missing piece that would always be missing would be their loved one.

For the grievers, the gift of completing the class was them being able to look at and accept all the other connected and assembled pieces that also made up their lives.

In the end, she gave hope and realization to the grievers. Their missing pieces, from time to time, would still evoke emotions, reminding them of their incomplete earthly puzzle. The gift and promise made to them was that their puzzle would be completed on the other side for time and all eternity.

As for Tami, in all the sessions she facilitated, there was one griever that forever changed her life in recognizing how his loss helped others.

At the beginning of the fall series and her first grief session, there was an attending griever that was an older gentleman. Alan had been the caretaker of his wife, who had suffered from Alzheimer's—a painful disease not only for the one who has it but also for Alan. Each passing day, Alan watched each of their precious memoires of their long life spent together die, yet the love of his life still lived.

During the continuation of Tami's continuing sessions, Alan confessed he found something that was helping him deal with his grief. It was to provide service to others.

Curious, she asked, "Alan, what are you doing in providing service to others?"

Happy for the opportunity to share with the group, he expounded, "The other day, I passed a man that was cutting down his tree with a handsaw. Stopping, I took a few minutes to talk to the man, and soon I found out that the handsaw was the only thing he could afford. I quickly asked if he would mind if I helped him, and he agreed.

"Telling the man I would be right back, I went home, got my chain saw, and returned to the man's house. Within no time, we had the tree cut down into manageable pieces so the man could also use it for firewood.

"I find that I feel the best when I am providing my service in helping people."

Grateful for Alan's input, Tami responded, "Alan, I am so happy you shared this with the group. Providing service to others not only helps them but also the person providing the service."

In all of Tami's grief series, as part of Tami's personality, she would greet each of the grief attendees at the beginning of the session; and at the end of the session, she would kindly demand a hug from everyone!

With each weekly class, Tami would invite a speaker that would share their specific knowledge about grief. Slowly, as each class progressed, piece by piece, each of the grievers began to understand themselves. One of the guest speakers, which Tami always had for the last class, used to say, "Grief is a feeling process, not a thinking process."

Tami and I loved the HBO Series *Six Feet Under*. It was about a family-owned funeral home.

In several classes, she had families that lost a child, and the paraphrased passage below (from the series) addressed the gravity of this loss and has stayed with us forever.

> When a woman loses her husband, she is a widow. When a man loses his wife, he is a widower. When a family loses a child, it is so ugly there is no name for it.

At the end of each class, as Tami drove home, she would talk about how much she worried about each attendee; and out of extreme compassion, she hurt deeply for each of them. Having suffered grief herself, she knew what it was like to walk in their shoes.

One of her guest speakers was a degreed therapist and confessed that after taking several courses in grief, he thought that he knew a lot about the subject; but after losing his mother, he realized he knew very little, not having experienced grief himself.

— 24 —

Not feeling very well for some time, Tami was experiencing pain in her lower abdomen. The diagnosis was that she had to have surgery to remove a growth that had amassed in the same area of her hysterectomy many years past.

As with all of Tami's surgeries, this one also took longer than expected; and to add to the severity of her condition, her doctor had to call in another doctor for help.

Her primary doctor, which was also a patient of Tami's, later told her, "The whole time we were cutting away the mass, the doctor helping me kept saying, 'This is cancer.'"

She was finished with the surgery, but after they took her off of the respirator, she was not breathing.

Meeting with us the next few days in the hospital and filling in the blanks on what happened, the doctor confessed, "When the anesthesiologist pulled out your breathing tube, he couldn't get you to start breathing on your own. He was working frantically. I have never seen an anesthesiologist work harder in getting the breathing tube inserted back down into your airway."

While being wheeled out of surgery, she lay on the gurney and was still on oxygen and groggy. I walked beside her as the attendants took her up to her room.

Staying with her for the next few days at her bedside, I was present when the oncologist came in and went over with us his report from the lab findings. To our relief, there was no cancer.

A few days later, she was released but was still not able to sustain a survivable blood oxygen saturation. With that, she would need portable oxygen tanks and a home oxygen concentrator until she recovered and was able to breathe on her own.

Tami got back to work, and within a few months, she was now free of her portable oxygen tank and hoses. She was feeling better than ever; and she, together with the best team she ever had, were now again setting monthly records at her store.

Tami used to boast, "Number four has always been my lucky number. I was the fourth daughter, born on the fourth day of the fourth month, and birthed the fourth grandchild, and my fourth husband is going to be so awesome!"

Since I was only husband number two, I always felt she had her work cut out for her to be able to reach husband number four as training new husbands is so hard and takes too long!

Also, part of her decision to become a manger of an existing store was easy. The store number was number four!

Every day while Tami was at work, at 4:44 PM, it was a race to see who could text "444" first as a way of communicating that we were thinking and expressing the love we had for each other. Of course, with me already home from work, the Vegas odds of me texting first and winning was about 85 percent of the time.

*****

As another year rolled around, Tami was now the leading manager as far as her earnings were concerned. She was on top of her game; and with her success and confidence, inevitably, from time to time, Tami, prompted from feeling overwhelming remorse and shame, would confess to me that she had, had an encounter with another man.

As for myself, I am ashamed to admit that I was involved with another woman. But it was not out of spite or revenge on Tami, as I loved her very much.

I was not being a player or ever looking. What started out as friendship eventually just happened.

For me, it was never about seeking love or a replacement as both she and I were married and very happily in love with our spouses.

For me, it was about trying to understand how my wife could compartmentalize while living with and loving me yet not be haunted by a guilty conscience. As for Tami, she masked having an encounter very well. On returning home, she would make up some story as to where she had been. With her wanting to believe it so much, she actually did by totally enforcing her will to believe while forcing out where she had actually been.

I often wondered why I could never find Tami's metaphorical USB brain port that she stored these memories on. More incredible was her ability to just replace the chip with a fresh, new chip and wipe out that memory.

But I do know why. At a very young age, she had to learn how to block the horrible *predatory* images and memories out of her mind just to survive, and that's how she survived. Regarding Tami's loving and living, a line from an old movie ("I'm just not going to think about it. I'll think about it tomorrow") summed up her thinking.

As for my first wife, Nancy, she eventually felt that neither I nor our three children were what she really wanted. She felt as if she had missed something in her life and somehow been robbed of having the chance to live a single life. Over time, her love for me had diminished, and she soon found replacements.

As for Tami, below is one of the texts she sent me.

> You asked me why I stayed, because I loved you, even when it was sometimes hard to like you…I thank God every day for you. You are a joy and a blessing in my life, I love you more than you'll ever know. Thanks for being my husband, my sweetheart, my everything.

In reality, Tami was never looking to replace me. Halfheartedly, you could almost say she was doing everything her mother told her not to do!

Tami could be reckless, almost daring for a reckoning of herself—a reckoning for being raped or even a reckoning for her past actions—yet still hoping for forgiveness from a higher deity.

Tami was a free spirit full of adventure and tested every aspect of her God-given gift of free agency.

For me, after I eventually found out, it wasn't the actual encounter that hurt me but the betrayal through the cover-up lies she told me.

As our marriage continued year after year and with me knowing Tami's dark past as a young teen, I came to believe that she was reaching from and reacting out of the collateral damage inflicted by her *predator*.

As for my affair, it eventually ended, and I told Tami what I had done.

Strangely, Tami reacted with jealously. With that, my reaction was that I was almost in disbelief. I silently thought, *Really? After all the encounters you've had?*

After a few days, Tami confessed she was almost relieved as it softened some of her guilt, and her willingness for forgiveness was immediate.

For me, the woman I was involved with was a very kind individual, and after it ended, what I learned afterward was that having an affair can and will damage so much.

In any marriage, when you are together, you and your spouse deserve to spend a great portion of your time, energy, and love with each other.

For me, a simple marriage math equation is this: you cannot be involved with someone else and not change its properties by diminishing or subtracting time in your married relationship. Any number subtracted by another number is less than the whole. As for Tami, she somehow defied this formula.

In the end, as I faced what I had done, destitution overwhelmed my soul. With Tami and I working together, both of our spirits deep down inside survived and healed through the power of forgiveness.

As for our marriage and the love we shared with each other, we made a commitment in our vows, and together it was until death do us part.

As time progressed, Tami's breathing symptoms slowly and steadily started to betray her, causing shortness of breath and occasional dizziness.

We were taking a weekend trip, and while dining at a restaurant, Tami was trying her hardest but could barely catch her breath and was on the verge of passing out. I helped her, and within a few short minutes, she had recovered but was still unsteady. Holding her close like I used to when she was recovering from the accident, I guided her out of the restaurant and helped her into the car. With the aid of fresh air, she soon recovered.

After going back to the hotel, we took the rest of the evening to just rest. One thing she also noticed over time was that she could no longer sleep on her left side.

We traveled back home, again with the altitude changes, and Tami vacillated between being able to breathe and struggling with shortness of breath.

Within a week, we made an appointment to see a specialist. But before we could make the appointment, I had to rush her to the emergency room as she was having trouble breathing again. Pulled away from Tami to give the hospital administrators their required information, I left her with the nurses to attend to her needs. In my absence, she passed out. On my return, she was taken to another room, and I quickly followed.

The hospital, contacting her yet-to-be-seen specialist, made the decision to admit Tami. Now Tami was in a wheelchair heading up to her room, and I walked by her side. Alert, she was very concerned as to where they were taking her. We soon passed a hospital directional sign reading Intensive Care. Scared, Tami quickly looked up at me.

I put my hand on her shoulder and softly spoke, "It's all right, baby. They just want to see what is causing your breathing problems so they can help you."

I stayed with Tami very late into the night. Her only attending physician, seemingly possessed, was determined to find answers and worked diligently throughout the night.

The next morning, the doctors announced that somewhere, somehow, for some unknown reason, Tami's phrenic nerve was no longer actuating the nerve signal to her left diaphragm. This was an integral part of subconscious breathing; this nerve causes the lungs to expand by pulling in oxygen. Once the phrenic nerve is damaged, you lose the lung, and there is no cure.

Tami was released from the hospital and was given and portable oxygen tank, and upon returning home, she would again have extra tanks and a home oxygen concentrator.

She was scheduled less than a week later with her specialist, and they would perform a test to measure how much air capacity the right lung was providing.

Going into a sterile room, Tami faced a strange object that almost resembled a rich man's old-school stand-up phone booth. Following a white coated technician, she trepidatiously approached the rectangular wood-framed glass box and carefully listened to the medical operator as he quickly parroted the procedure instructions.

After nervously sitting down, the operator closed the door, and all the room's background noises suddenly grew silent. The technician quickly disappeared into the control room, and suddenly the machine slowly started sucking all the oxygen out of the sealed container as its sole purpose was to measure the volume capacity of the right lung.

I met Tami soon after the test, and she told me the test caused her to experience extreme panic and terror. Feeling as if she was again in the hands of her childhood predator, she was slowly being suffocated while getting the needed data.

A few days later, we met with the specialist, and the results he revealed to us were bad. He knew the left lung was not going to be part of the equation as it had 0 percent volume but had hoped the percentage for the right lung would be high. Sadly and horribly, it was not so. Her right lung only had 30 percent volume, which meant Tami would be oxygen dependent for the rest of her life.

For me, there were no words to describe the pain I was feeling for Tami. When we first started dating, I knew, as did she, that she had always suffered in coping with lung trouble from various causes.

As for Tami, sad and disappointed, she always drew from what her grandmother used to tell her as a young child: "You can either laugh or cry, but crying will only give you a headache."

Going through our life together, we lived on love, hope, and good will. Drawing comfort, we knew the most important thing we had was each other.

After a few months, one Sunday morning, Tami was lying in bed when she turned to me and said, "I have thought it over. I want to get a dog."

I smiled, knowing the tone of her voice. I lovingly said, "That would be nice. I know how much you love dogs, and you have been missing having one."

After getting dressed, I went out to the front yard and started mowing. Looking up, I saw Tami sitting on the veranda, talking on the phone. I mowed for a few minutes more. Smiling, Tami motioned for me to come over.

I stopped and walked over, and before I could speak, she exclaimed, "I made an appointment at eleven o'clock for us to go see a breeder! She has two crossbred female Shih-poo puppies! I want to go to the pet store and buy what we need before we pick one out!"

Smiling, supportive, and upbeat, I happily replied, "I'll go put the mower away!

We pulled up to the house and greeted the breeder, and they soon led us out to the backyard, to a small fenced-in area. There the mother and her two remaining puppies were playing. Both puppies were rambunctious. One was all white, and the other was full of color, ranging from predominantly dark champagne to the stark blending of a black face and two white front paws.

Tami, excited, glanced at me. "Which one do you think?"

I looked at the all-white puppy. I thought the white color would be a distraction because of the possibility of the dog's discoloration from eye stains.

Leaning over, I whispered, "Tami, get the female with the most color. Her markings are very unique, and I love how she is looking at us."

Turning to the breeder in excitement, she exclaimed, "We'll take the beige one!"

The breeder, hoping we would have chosen the white one, shot a concerned look to her husband, queried, "Jon, I know in your heart, you wanted to keep the beige one for breeding. What do you think?"

Jon looked at the two puppies. He then turned to look at Tami. I did not actually see Tami's facial expression, but knowing her, I would think that she was throwing some serious puppy-dog eyes to Jon, hoping he would let her have the one she wanted.

Jon smiled at Tami. "It's okay. She can have the beige one!"

As we were driving home, Tami, happy, suddenly announced she would name the puppy Lilly Belle after the Disneyland train coach that Walt Disney built and named after his wife.

Tami wanted to stop by her parents'. It was as if she was a teenager again. She was so excited to show off her new puppy!

When she returned to work, to her relief, both her staff and her patients were happy to have her back and helped her adjust to what Tami soon labeled her oxygen contraption: her nose-hose leash.

Later in the year, we wanted a more updated system as changing the tanks at work was much too often and always cumbersome since we were on five liters of oxygen. We purchased a battery-powered concentrator, and even though she still had to pull it behind her, the batteries were easier and quicker to change. Besides, in Tami's mind, she felt it made her look less old and feeble.

26

We were approaching our twenty-fifth-anniversary getaway. This was going to be the longest time for us to be away from the closeness and emergency backup options of oxygen supplies.

Because of the high volume of oxygen needed to providing her life support, I always made sure there was a backup plan. This entailed having the portable oxygen concentrator as it had a 12-volt adapter for the car and plenty of spare batteries. For our hotel room, we brought the home concentrator, which reinvigorated her while she slept, providing a continuous five-liter oxygen supply. We also packed eight large and eight small oxygen tanks as the final emergency backup plan. I also brought along an emergency backpack, which had a small oxygen tank and a hose incase the battery concentrator ceased working.

We rented a van, picked up our two girls and our two grand-daughters' daughters in Vegas, and drove to San Diego. Returning to some of the same places where our marriage began was so special for us.

We went to San Diego Wild Animal Park, LEGOLAND, and SeaWorld, and we also brought along a wheelchair.

Among everything Tami had to accept and adapt to, the wheelchair was the hardest for her. Throughout her life, her freedom to come and go and do what she wanted to do whenever she wanted to do it was paramount. As for me, pushing the wheelchair was rough at times, especially when navigating the uneven terrain at the wild animal park.

What became a welcome relief for Tami was the fact that at sea level, oxygen is at its highest level. This greatly helped her breath and stay oxygenated.

The best part of the trip was Grandma being able to see and be close to our oldest and youngest grandchildren, watching them experience and see new things and having so much fun, especially at LEGOLAND and San Diego Zoo.

Going back to the same restaurant where we had our first romantic honeymoon dinner was hard for us. On our honeymoon, so youthful and full of life, we held hands as we walked up the stairs to the dining room. Twenty-five years later, now with Tami wheelchair bound, we were guided to the service elevator to be taken upstairs, which was hard for both of us.

After so many years of special memories, it was a miracle the restaurant had retained its name. Sadly, we realized that not only had things changed for us but also the restaurant. The venue and atmosphere had also all changed. Instead of Tami and me again recapturing our romantic, intimate moments with our daughters and granddaughters, sadly, time had marched on. The once personal and quiet restaurant was now loud and impersonable.

At SeaWorld, Jaxson, our soon-to-be son-in-law, joined us. We all had a good time watching the grandkids enjoy the killer whales, sea lions, and all the other aquatic exhibits.

We said goodbye to Mary, Jaxson, and Amanda in San Diego, and Catherine and Samantha stayed with us as we returned to Vegas and stayed with them an extra day to give Tami time to rest.

For the remaining week of our vacation, we visited all of Southern Utah's national parks, where we relaxed and enjoyed just being together.

As we were driving back home, I could tell the higher we got in altitude, the quieter and more tired she became.

No sooner had we gotten back from San Diego than, four months later, we packed all of Tami's oxygen gear and made our way to Sacramento for Mary and Jaxson's wedding.

After having lived in Vegas for the longest time, Greg and Linnea had moved to the small farming town where they grew up together.

Having never been to their new house, we stopped by for a visit and rest, but most importantly, it was to spend some time with them. Greg and Linnea took us everywhere as Tami, happy, flourished from being so close to sea level. We enjoyed our time immensely. They showed us the surrounding farm areas; and we were treated to seeing the local agriculture, consisting of walnut trees, fruit trees, and, to our amazement, kiwis.

We soon had to leave, but we were lucky enough to be able to visit with them again as they were also invited to the wedding.

Mary and Jaxson, in their long search for just the right venue, picked a ranch in Sacramento that was specifically designed to accommodate country-style ranch weddings that included cabins for the guests.

On the day of the wedding, all of Mary's entourage was busy having a party while they prepared their hair and makeup for the wedding.

As for the men, they were treated to skeet shooting with shotguns.

Teasing Jaxson, I commented, "Nothing makes a wedding more interesting and certain than having a few shotguns around!"

It was a perfect afternoon. Even my former wife, Nancy, was in attendance. Mary would have no one else officiate her wedding except the one who continually believed in her, fought for and with her, and loved her, and that was her mom…Tami.

All the guests were seated. This was the second time I got to escort our youngest daughter, Mary, down the aisle. With Catherine's wedding and pursuant to her request, Tami also walked with us down the aisle.

I was trying to hold back my tears of joy, and Mary pleaded, "Dad, don't you cry because you will make me cry."

Sitting down, I took a few moments to enjoy seeing Mary so happy and Tami glowing with joyful pride that the teenager we sometimes wanted to kill had turned out to be such a beautiful and loving daughter.

Tami started the ceremony. Throughout the year of preparation and venue researching, Mary, on Facebook, blended her and Jaxson's names to Mason. Not meaning to, Tami slipped at the beginning and called them Mason, and the whole wedding party broke into laughter!

They had prepared a wonderful ceremony, and Tami still and always impressed me with her oratory skills, which reflected her pure honesty and love.

Bringing their families closer together, Jaxson, standing in front of Amanda, brought her and everyone else to tears on the promises and opportunity to be involved in her life.

To my surprise, I was also very blessed and happy to have my best friend, Gene (from Chicago), to be there to share our happiness. Always having fun with people, Gene, mingling with the guests, portrayed himself as a neighbor living down the road that would frequent the various wedding events as the wedding crasher.

The reception party extended well into the night and into the early-morning hours. Suddenly and abruptly, the owners of the facility showed up and intervened, demanding it to end!

Driving home, we again stopped to rest Greg and Linnea's and once again enjoyed their company.

We drove the rest of the way home. Tami, for the most part, was rested but was so happy to be a part of something so wonderful.

After returning to work, within a few months, Tami worried that she was beginning to lose the use of her hands.

The doctor that performed the neck fusion, as part of our debriefing, told me that part of his procedure was to take the surrounding bone spurs, grind the bone spurs into a paste, and fill in and around the two plates.

This was my summation of the operation four years since, considering my understanding of the procedure: I was always suspicious and worried that the bone paste would start taking on a life of its own. With that, the nerves encased inside Tami's upper spinal cord would start getting squeezed, thus causing her hands to lose feeling and strength.

To help her, I started to do all household chores, including the laundry and cooking, to help her just rest.

Work was getting harder; and one morning, calling me and in tears, Tami said couldn't button up her pants. Stopping by my work, I helped her out. I then gave her a loving kiss and a hug. It hurts so bad to see the one person in your life that you love so much be in such pain and anguish, and you are *helpless* to fix it.

— 27 —

As the months passed, Tami's only functional lung was getting weaker, and she was losing even more control of her hands.

Seeing both her physical and psychological attributes diminishing, together we reached an agreement. Knowing she could no longer work, we would need to sell our house and downsize.

In the interim, we would move in with Tami's parents, now in their eighties, to help take care of them.

Selling our house quickly, we signed contracts the week after Christmas. We were given three weeks to move, and our two daughters and Jaxson came up to help us one weekend. The rest of the time, Tami helped as much as she could as I stayed very busy packing. Toward the end, the only thing left to put into the storage sheds was our furniture.

On the final two days, together we moved in with her parents. After getting the spare bedroom in order, we could now sleep there.

The following day, the bishop and our ward all got together; and with many hands, we finished moving all the furniture within three hours.

On the last day, with the help of one of Tami's sisters, we bagged all the food and took it over to Tami's parents' house.

Alone at the end on the last day of ownership, I took a few minutes to say goodbye. Pausing at each room, I relived some of the thousands of precious memories Tami and I shared over our fourteen years of living there. Wiping away a few tears, I closed the front door for the final time. I then pulled out of the driveway, closing the chapter on one part of our lives. I was grateful for our incredible journey and memories.

As I was parking in front of Tami's parents' house, I immediately knew something was going on from the number of cars parked there.

I walked into the house, and I went to her parents' bedroom, where Tami, all the sisters, and their husbands had gathered. With me now here, the group was complete.

I had missed all that had been said to each of the sisters and their husbands, and when Imara saw I was there, she spent a few minutes telling me how much she loved me and also all the help, respect, and support I had given her throughout the years.

Grateful, I shared my feelings. "Mom, thank you. You are also very special to me. I will always be grateful for you taking care of my mom in her last few days on Earth and how special you made her feel."

Wanting to lighten our moment together, I continued, "When you get to heaven, tell my mom and dad I love them. And, oh, by the way, don't let my mom push you around!"

With Mom finished saying her goodbyes, she lay down to rest as the room emptied.

Within a few days, Mom was gone and not from any failing medical condition. She died very tired as she had fought a good fight and lived a good and righteous life in the service of God and His Son, Jesus Christ.

In my whole life, I had never witnessed anyone lying down and just willing themselves to die peacefully.

I will always remember us being the first to arrive at the funeral home to see Mom. Composed and grateful, Tami lovingly touched up her mother's hair.

At the funeral, each sister was to take no more than fifteen minutes to speak, starting from oldest to youngest. Tami was last.

Dragging her oxygen concentrator, she proceeded up to the podium.

Out of breath, she teasingly remarked, "Well, there goes my fifteen minutes just getting up here!"

As the crowd's laugh subsided, Tami continued.

Sitting in the pew again, as I had done many years ago at Dirk's funeral, I sat amazed as she eulogized her mother.

So raw and so real, her heart encapsulated the love and kindness she had for her mother and what a patient and good example she was to her.

Poking fun at herself, Tami interjected, "Even in the years that I didn't listen to her, I did what I wanted to do, either good or bad, anyway! But one thing she did do was she never gave up on me and was always proud of me. That is what a mom is supposed to do."

With Imara gone, Tami's job was just to keep an eye on Bob. She did this until I got home from work, and I would fix lunch and, later on in the day, dinner.

I also did the laundry, and as a relief, the sisters had a cleaning service come in to clean the house once a week.

*****

As the months flew by, Tami continued to falter. Coming home, she asked if I would wash her hair, which I lovingly did.

With Tami's birthday and our anniversary coming up, she arranged for us and the girls along with their families to go to Disneyland.

We had extra money from the sale of our house, and it was always Tami's dream to stay at Disneyland Hotel.

Happy for her and wanting her to have her wish, I was both touched and happy when watching her make the reservations!

With the sisters working out a rotation schedule to take care of their dad, we left to travel and stay at Catherine's house for one night to rest before venturing on to "the Happiest Place on Earth."

Again, with traveling and the changes in altitude, it was hard for Tami to keep her oxygen saturation stabilized.

Finally reaching sea level, as we approached Riverside, Tami was tired, but thankfully, she was starting to get some relief.

We pulled up to Disneyland Hotel, and the hotel staff could not have been more kind or helpful.

As I checked in, Tami waited in one of the lobby's Mad Hatter teacups. Tired, happy, and content, she smiled at the guests walking by, which also brought a grateful and happy smile to my face.

We walked back outside and saw that Tami's electric mobility scooter had been delivered. With the help of guest services, they retrieved it, and she was able to ride it to our room. We had learned from our San Diego anniversary trip. Since Tami wanted to be free-spirited and independent, the scooter not only let her enjoy her freedom but also held her portable oxygen concentrator.

Shortly after our arrival to our room, the valet brought up all our luggage and the home oxygen concentrator. We set it up. Tami was now on constant oxygen as we waited for the kids to arrive.

The next morning, all of us met for breakfast. Everyone was so happy to be together on an adventure that had encapsulated almost twenty-eight years of happiness and memories.

We stopped first on Main Street. Tami was so overjoyed in seeing Samantha get so excited to see Minnie Mouse.

Venturing on, we then went to Tami's favorite ride, the Jungle Cruise. Samantha was excited to be on a boat and see all the animals. Who could ever forget the thrill of seeing the Backside of Water!

One nice thing about staying at the hotel was being able to walk everywhere at the park and having the hotel close by for resting.

One night, the kids and grandkids decided to stay later, so we headed back to our room first. For no particular reason, Tami was in a hurry. I literally had to run to keep up with her.

I was running out of energy; and with what breath I had left, I asked if she could slow down, which she did.

Our last day in Disneyland was melancholy with nobody wanting to say anything but all subconsciously knowing our adventure was almost over. I remember the pure joy of Tami watching the afternoon parade and loving the characters from the movie *Up* as she gleamed at Russell, who was riding on the back of the elusive bird he named Kevin.

We had our last family breakfast at Disneyland Hotel. It was fun to see the grandkids have so much fun seeing the characters.

With the cars all packed up, we were ready to leave. Taking our last family pictures in front of Mickey Mouse statue under the canopy by the main hotel entrance was truly memorable.

With Tami and I driving out, we were able to wave to Mary, Jaxson, and Amanda one last time as we drove away.

❦ 28 ❧

For the next few months of taking care of Bob, several times during the night, I was awakened by the sound of him falling. After getting up, I would go into his bedroom to see if he was hurt or needed any emergency medical attention. Not needing any medical assistance, I lifted Bob, who wouldn't help himself, and not having anyone to help me, both times, I used all my strength to pick him up, which felt like lifting deadweight, and get him back to bed.

With Tami wanting desperately to be able to see her newest grandchild, Mary took it upon herself to call James, telling him Mom was not doing good and that if he wanted to see her, to please come up with his family.

Within a few weeks, they did come up to visit, and we enjoyed every minute of our time with them.

When we went to Park City, I was glad James and his wife, Janice, were with us as they helped relieve me from pushing Tami's wheelchair up the steep hills of the main thoroughfare street.

As time passed, Tami had now reached a point where she needed more care and help. In some of our conversations, from time to time, she would share her knowledge as to where she hid certain valuable items in her parents' house.

A few days before our anniversary, Tami asked, "The anniversary present I bought us arrived today! Do you want to see it?"

Touched that my love had bought us a present, I softly replied, "That was so thoughtful, Tami! Let's wait a few more days until it's is the actual day so we can open it up together!"

We left on a Friday to pick up our granddaughter for two weeks. To make it easier, we would stop and stay at a motel to let Tami rest, and then we would venture on next day to meet Catherine and pick up Samantha.

On the first leg of the trip, Tami was paying one of our bills using her phone. After she finished, she said, "Now, if you ever need to know how to pay this bill and the password you need to have, I have it all here in my notes in my phone."

It's funny how the mind works as denial and unequivocal hope invade reality. Like a typical man, her words passed in one ear and out the other as my brain convinced itself, *What I think I heard, I heard. But no, I don't need to know that. I can't face that.*

When I woke up the next morning, Tami was in bad shape. Her oxygen saturation was at 86 percent. Sitting her up, I begged for her to take deep breaths while I kept monitoring her saturation. It climbed to 92 percent, and we started on the second leg of our journey.

Meeting up with Catherine, her husband Mick, and Samantha, we had lunch.

Still in bad shape, Tami made the best of it. Finished with lunch, together we gathered all of Samantha's luggage and put them in our car.

We said goodbye and put Samantha in her car seat, in the middle of the back seat. Grandma sat next to her so she could visit and entertain her.

On our way back, I continually kept an eye on Tami using the rearview mirror. Several times she would nod off, then I would call out her name, and she would jolt back up. After having this happen a few times, I pulled over and hooked up one of the oxygen tanks. To help her, I set the oxygen supply at a constant five liters, which helped revive her. The downside of her portable concentrator was that it only puffed five liters of concentrated oxygen when she inhaled.

When we arrived home, Tami was exhausted, and we learned Bob had taken a turn for the worse. After cheating death many times in his life, this time could be it.

After unpacking the car, I played with Samantha outside and then started dinner.

One sister was still at the house. Finished with her shift in caring for her dad and getting ready to leave, she met me in the kitchen.

The sister started the conversation. "I can't believe Tami brought Samantha here to take care of her with Dad being in his condition."

Understanding the stress everyone was going through, I calmly replied, "This could be the last time Tami has the opportunity to be with her granddaughter, so whatever happens, Tami spending time with her grandchild needs to happen."

Throughout all of Tami's life, she would always help anyone with only one exception: Tami herself.

It was Sunday morning, and with Samantha sleeping well, I ran to the store.

While Tami was resting, she heard knocking at the front door. Tami instinctively knew it was the elders in her father's ward bringing the sacrament.

Tami prayed as hard as she could, *My Lord,* please *give me the strength to make it to the door to be able to take the* sacrament. God, I need and want *to take the* sacrament.

With all her remaining strength, she made it and was able to take the sacrament.

In all of Tami's life, her love for her Savior was always deep in her heart. In the times where Tami was weak and faltered, she took personal ownership of her sins and the grace of Christ's sacrifice. As our spirits ascend into heaven, *He* takes away the sins of the world in the blessed *hope* of us receiving God's forgiveness.

Oftentimes Tami would confess to me, "I feel so remorseful and guilty for the pain and anguish I caused Jesus in the Garden of Gethsemane. Jesus, fulfilling His passion, was crucified and died for my sins. He did this for me so I could be saved and to return to Him."

With Bob now actively dying, his daughters wanted to stay with their father. Two of the sisters stayed with him so he would not die alone. The sisters also stayed to greet the visiting members of the ward who were coming in and out of the house to pay their last respects.

I was getting ready to put Samantha to bed, but the plan of having her sleep in the living room was clearly an option that was not going to work.

Tami was already in bed, and I brought Samantha into our bedroom for her to watch her while I went to take a bath.

After returning, I lay in bed as I read Samantha a story until she slowly fell asleep. I crawled out of bed, concerned about Tami, and softly asked, "How are you feeling?"

Spent, she softly answered, "I feel tired. But I am okay."

Taking her oxygen saturation, I replied, "Hey, ninety-six!"

Smiling, softly Tami said, "Oh…that's good!"

Leaving, I turned to see her on the right side of the bed, Lilly Belle in the center, and Samantha on the left. I turned out the light and shut the door.

Still uneasy, I made my bed on the living room couch as the visitors continued to arrive and depart. Somewhere around 10:00 PM, I fell asleep.

29

After waking up in the morning, I passed our bedroom door and saw the two sisters sitting by the foot of Bob's bed, talking, as I went into the bathroom.

Walking back into our bedroom, I turned on the light. I saw Tami lying on the carpeted floor, on her left side, her back toward me.

Walking in a little farther, I saw Samantha lying crossways on the bed. Looking down at Tami, I tenderly thought, *Oh, Tami. Samantha crowded you out of bed, so you slept on the floor.*

I got on my knees and felt her arm. It was cold. Suddenly I noticed she did not have her oxygen on.

I tried to find her oxygen hose nosepiece, then tried to roll her so I could put it on her.

Not able to get the hose from under her, I jumped to my feet and ran into the sisters, exclaiming, "Tami is in trouble! Call 911!"

I ran back, still frantically trying to get Tami's hose. One sister came in with the 911 operator on the speaker.

I rolled Tami on her back and, for the first time, saw a powdery white substance mixed with blood that had expelled from her nose.

The operator told us to start CPR, and we both took turns.

Desperate, I knew she also needed oxygen. I opened Tami's mouth and tried to breathe in the breath of life, forcing in my breath. I was immediately met with stiff resistance in trying to get any needed air into her only functioning lung.

I heard sirens approaching, and somehow someone let them in. The paramedics asked us to leave. I remember Lilly growling at them as both the sister and I were asked leave.

Sitting in the hallway, I watched as the paramedics worked feverishly, trying to revive Tami.

Finally, one of the paramedics stepped out. In a low, solemn voice, he said, "I am so sorry, sir. She was too far gone for us to revive her."

The sudden shock from the finality of something I had terrifyingly dreaded for so long had come to pass as the numbness of disbelief overtook my soul.

I was still in the hallway when the police arrived, and one officer took me into the bathroom. After closing the door, he began to ask the questions he needed to ask. He had a microphone for his two-way radio, which was attached to his bandolier, and it also recorded my testimony. The officer's questions seemed unending and repetitive as the only thing of importance to me was calling and telling our daughters the horrific news before Tami's sisters did.

Getting a break between questions, I sincerely asked, "Officer, I have to call our two daughters now as I want to tell them of their mother's passing and not my wife's sisters."

Calling Catherine first, I did my best in telling her that her mother had just passed away. I don't remember much of what was said, but what I do remember is the horrific screaming and crying. And then I started crying as I repeatedly apologized for her loss, saying, "I'm sorry. I'm sorry. I'm so sorry."

I then called Mary and told her, her mother had passed away. Again, as with Catherine, Mary let out a horrific scream followed by inconsolable crying. I also was crying and again expressing my sorrow for their loss.

I hung up the phone. After recomposing, I again turned my attention to answering the officer's questions.

Finished with one, I moved to the living room. I was now retelling my story to an officer of a higher rank.

While talking with the officer, I noticed unknown people walking in and out of the house. Little did I know that the police went to see Tami's doctor to see if they could get them to sign a death certificate. However, Tami's physician assistant was out of town, and the other doctors would not sign off on the death certificate.

The officer was just about completed with me, so I asked the officer if I could see Tami again before they took her away. He agreed.

With the medical personnel finished, they led me in to see her. Tami was already in a body bag, and the only exposed part of her I could see was her face, below which the zipper stopped. Not knowing what I could and could not do, I spent a few minutes just looking at her. I had also just lost my life by losing the love of my life.

I called the two boys. They were sad, upset, and in shock and asked me as soon as possible to give them the details concerning the funeral arrangements so they could schedule their families' flights.

One surprise visitor was one of the funeral directors from the mortuary Tami worked at. Always very kind and loving to both of us, he told me it would be an honor for him to take care of all the arrangements.

Grateful for his help, I knew he would take good care of Tami.

One of my last two calls was to Travis, telling him of Tami's passing.

The other call was to my best friend, Gene, in Chicago, and he assured me he would be there.

To add to the day, later on in the afternoon, I was in the living room, entering data in my phone, among all other things I needed to do. Looking up, I watched unknown personnel wheel Bob out, who, unknowingly to me, had passed away sometime in the afternoon.

Now the family was planning two different funerals. On Friday, I had to leave halfway through Bob's to go pick up Gene at the airport.

While we were on the way to drop him off at his hotel, Gene said the most peculiar thing to me that at first, when he said it, I thought, *Gene, that was kind of cold.* But in reality, it was the most profound and true advice I had ever heard: "You will never get over it. But you will get through it."

All the kids were in town, and they were all able to be at their mom's viewing on Friday evening.

Seeing her for the first time, I was able to spend some time with her alone. It was both peacefully surreal and hard to accept the finality of a loss of someone that was my whole life.

After getting through it, we all went back to the hotel to be together.

Saturday morning was the day of her funeral. One of my requests to the four kids and our one pseudo daughter was to put the fun in the word *funeral* as that was what she would have wanted.

Attendees were filling up the ward pews, and the overflow seating was also utilized for the mourners—except there weren't many sad moments.

One by one, our kids got up and made the attendees laugh, telling their many memories of their mom's antics and actions and a life that touched and forever changed and influenced their lives.

Years later, Tami's best friend told me it was the funniest and happiest funeral she had ever been to as it encapsulated the tender Tami, with the stories that needed to be told and would have made her very happy.

I also spoke of a few funny Tami antics, but in the end, I quoted a few lines from the song Tami dearly loved, "The Dance," which encapsulated how we felt about each other.

And now I'm glad I didn't know
The way it all would end
The way it all would go
Our lives are better left to chance
I could have missed the pain
But I'd have had to miss the dance

Starting to cry a little, I ended with "Thank you, Tami…for the dance."

We mirrored something the mortuary used to do each year that Tami would participate in. We replicated it. Since Memorial Day was on Monday, Tami was to be buried on Tuesday.

With the crowd following Tami's casket out to the coach, our kids, our beloved bishop, and I helped take all the colorful helium balloons outside. We distributed the balloons and passed out indelible markers. The attendees wrote their personal memories on the balloons. We gave a balloon to everyone who wanted one and time to write a memory. All at once, everyone released them. They colorfully filled the sky as the coach carrying Tami slowly left the church.

I can't remember what I wrote, but I will always remember seeing the balloons through tear-filled eyes. Also, at that moment, what I did know was that Tami would have been so happy for the love that everyone showed to her.

On Saturday, our youngest son, Peter, made a request that his lapel flower be a bird-of-paradise. True to our family's humor, I arranged for it to happen, and Peter proudly wore it as a pallbearer on Tuesday, with immediate family in attendance.

With all our immediate family going home, the sisters were gracious enough to allow me to stay until I found a place of my own.

Staying the first night and the many nights afterward was hard. With that, finding an apartment was at the top of the list. With the help of a leasing agent, I was able to secure a one-year lease on an apartment. When she called me to tell me the good news, I cried. To this very day, we are still close friends and have lunch together from time to time.

Peter, wanting to help, came and helped me move out of the house and set up the TV and all other electronics via Wi-Fi, which was a tremendous help.

The one and only unexpected gift that came out of losing Tami was my brother. We were never really close. We went through the motions, but that was all. After hearing of my loss, he called me. I let him talk for a few minutes; and when we got to my turn, I told him I didn't care if he came or not as in my life, he had never really been there for me. So why start now?

Shocked, my brother apologized, and he and his wife attended the funeral. True to his word, he did make amends as he calls me almost every Thursday to see how I am doing.

One godsend was having Tami's friend Kate and her husband, Christopher, help us out with anything that we needed when we moved out of our house. Christopher and his son, Max, also came to my rescue in helping me move all of the furniture into the apartment.

Finally, I was in the apartment. Everything was there to make it a home—except Tami.

Below is one of Tami's last texts to me.

> Laying here counting my blessing. Two of the world's best husbands were given to me. 12 years of pure happiness and joy with Dirk and almost 26 years with Gary, who spoils me rotten and makes sure I feel loved and appreciated every day. I have truly been blessed…4 amazing children and now 6 of the sweetest, cutest, smartest, and all-around wonderful grandchildren in the world. It's no wonder I thank God for giving me so much.

⌁ 30 ⌁

Providing temporary relief from missing Tami, I kept myself busy with work. I also worked on turning my apartment into a home. I wanted it to not only reflect my life and my likings but also include Tami. The primary theme I wanted to project was in pictures celebrating our life together.

Throughout the years, having attended all of Tami's grief sessions, I found they helped, but the one thing I soon realized was that no two people grieve the same. Life is with the living, but not having Tami in my life left a tremendous void. I miss a lot of things about her, but the one thing I miss the most was her being my rock and sounding board in vetting out how to handle the feelings and dynamics with friends, family, coworkers, and acquaintances.

I was drawn more to likening myself to a hammer. I perceived most things as if they were a nail. Sadly, so unlike Tami, I lacked the gift of finesse and getting the right timing for decisions, which still continue to haunt me, confuse me, and get me in trouble.

As our marriage got on in years, Tami was the lead keel in my life that kept me upright and balanced. No matter how hard the wind blew, she always helped me balance out my life.

My one regret in losing the love of my life is I didn't get a chance to say goodbye. Every day I helped her live one more day. To make her life a little easier, I did everything I could to help her with the hope we would have just one more tomorrow.

One of the things I admired most about her is she lived her life as if there was no tomorrow. Me, on the other hand, I spent my whole life in "Tomorrow Land" and was much too busy to enjoy "Today Land."

I recently read a profound statement: "Live today because your last day on Earth only comes once in a lifetime and always the day before tomorrow."

In my bedroom, I put up a cork pin map of the United States and put colored pinheads on every place Tami and I had traveled.

When I was finished sticking the pins in, I could see we had been to thirty-three states and 118 places including DC, Hawaii, and Mexico. We also piloted and sailed both the Atlantic and the Pacific oceans.

In our twenty-seven years of marriage, we lived a life full of love and adventure. With that, many times in our marriage, we were broke, living from hand to mouth.

I know many people who save for the proverbial rainy day that eventually comes but not financially. The unexpected rainy day would come as a downpour of grief from the loss of their spouse and never having really traveled throughout their marriage.

It was a horrible injustice, losing Tami at the young age of fifty-six years old. Even more tragic was to have missed so many travel memories, and the only thing to show for it was a fat mattress full of money.

With Tami and me, as far as stuffing money in our mattress is concerned, it was continually overdrawn…but it was well used in making love!

A testament to a commitment full of love and adventures is knowing no boundaries. I know Tami is gone. But in my heart, she is still alive. Still so deeply in love with Tami, I could never surrender my heart to another woman because it would be a terrible injustice to her as I could never fully give her my heart.

Soon after Tami passed away, I remembered her one purpose in coming back from heaven: "You have to go back and help Gary become a better person." Going back to church at our ward, I also started going to a Catholic church. At one time, I was going to both denominations on Sundays.

I loved the LDS church and the people, so it was a hard choice. But there were too many memories; and the songs, although spiritual, were now bittersweet for me to hear.

Getting baptized in the Catholic faith, I was not closing a door to my prior faith or knowledge but opening the door wider to God and Jesus Christ. During the year where I took my baptismal classes, after many years trying to reach my goal, I finally read the Bible in its entirety.

At peace in my soul, I had finally broken through the many years of Tami trying to help me become a better person. Even though I have come far, I am still not done yet.

Attending Mary's baby shower, I had a chance to sit down and talk to Nancy. Feeling the need to apologize, humbly I started, "You know, in losing Tami, I have looked back at all my actions and short-comings involving us. The night you told me about the affair you had early on in our marriage, with me being so young, I was so crushed. What I lacked then was the maturity or the words that I could have used in trying to save our marriage. My biggest sin was harboring my feelings of betrayal and not letting the affair go. But my most egregious sin was not forgiving you."

"The questions I should have asked were 'Do you love him?' 'What do I need to do to change and save our marriage?' 'What do you need to do to save our marriage?' and 'Do you even want to try and save our marriage?'" Finished, I looked at Nancy.

She was silent for a moment. She began going through all my shortcomings as if they were items on a shopping list.

Listening intently, I would, from time to time, interrupt to say sincerely, "I'm sorry." With Nancy finished, I calmly and respectfully replied, "I understand, and I am guilty. Most of all, I can't turn the clock back, and for that, I am, again, sorry. I learned an interesting concept that by no means excuses my actions. It is 'You don't know what you don't know.' If what happened to us back then happened to us now, the outcome might have been different as I would know what to do, and that is to forgive and forget."

As for Tami's encounters with other men, reactions from some would be numerous, a number of them asking, "Why did you put up with it?"

Each one of us here today will at one time
in our lives look upon a loved one who is in need

and ask the same question: We are willing to help, Lord, but what, if anything, is needed? For it is true, we can seldom help those closest to us. Either we don't know what part of ourselves to give or, more often than not, the part we have to give is not wanted. And so it is those we live with and should know who elude us. But we can still love them—we can love completely without complete understanding. (Norman Maclean, *A River Runs through It*)

Getting help, I went to a counselor and asked, "Why did Tami get involved with other men?"

After I told him about Tami's background, with her being raped so violently and being so young, he said, "Among the married women I see and have gone through what your wife went through, the majority of these women, being victims of rape and molestation, also have fidelity issues, getting sexually involved with other men. Today's statistics say that one in four girls and one in nine boys are sexually molested."

One thing that was so hard for me to understand was how Tami could be with someone else and, on her way home, be able to compartmentalize her thoughts and emotions by putting them aside as she pulled into our garage. After many years since Tami's passing, I figured it out in very simple terms. The men Tami met to have sex with? It was just sex—a temporary high that somehow satisfied her sexual addition.

Tami always came back home to me because we had a history together. We had a life together and we loved each other very much.

In the end, it didn't matter what Tami ever did by her actions. What mattered was how she made me feel. And to the end, I felt *loved* and *appreciated*.

With my love so deep, I stood by her and fought for her.

Most of all, my first marriage failed because I could not forgive. My second marriage was saved because I learned how to forgive.

A woman's heart is a deep ocean of secrets. Tami said to me one time, "You know more about me than I have ever let anyone else know about me."

Falling in love is easy. Staying in love takes love and commitment. But most of all, individuals that harbor and pass judgment miss so many opportunities and the chance to drop their anchor and learn the true depth of God's grace.

To answer the question "Why did I put up with it?" it's because she was worth it!

The only person that made a difference in my life after Tami passed was my best friend, Gene.

While Tami was still alive, I had to cancel our planned trip to Cuba because of her health.

After Tami passed, we did get to meet up in Boston. As she was a Red Sox fan, she always wanted to take me there. With Gene and his friend Larry, I was able to go to a game and also a private tour of Fenway the following day.

Always wanting to go to New Orleans, I met Gene there and got to experience the food and the bayou, which included seeing plenty of alligators. The nightlife was crazy as it was best to be just an observer to the Bourbon Street regalia and never-ending spirits than a participant. At least you'd feel better in the morning!

I wanted to return to San Diego to celebrate what would have been our thirtieth anniversary, and our oldest granddaughter accompanied me. We stayed at the same hotel. It was a truly remarkable and memorable three days as we revisited the many places that made us so happy.

I have also visited our daughter Mary in San Jose many times, but the most special time was to see the birth of their daughter that carries Tami's middle name, Faye.

Our son Peter and his family have hosted me many times. A close, special family, they treated me to something I had always wanted to do, and that was to go up in a hot-air balloon in Albuquerque during Christmas.

Our son James and his family, living in Oceania, Virginia, have hosted me many times, and I got to revisit Cape Hatteras Lighthouse. Tami and I went there together with my mom.

I spent several Christmases with Catherine's family and helped them pack their house. They are now living in Denmark.

The one trip that was like no other trip I have ever taken was when Gene and I went to Iceland. When I first suggested it, Gene was skeptical, so I asked him to call James and Janice as they have been there many times.

Convinced, Gene was on board, and we went.

Gene has taught me many things in my life, but the most important lesson on something that I subconsciously knew but he accentuated into my consciousness was that to get the maximum out of life, you *never take the guided tour.*

In Iceland, we got to hike up to and onto a glacier. As I stood there, looking over where we had come but also where we were standing, tears filled my eyes, knowing Tami could also see.

As my life is continuing, I am not cast away but on a long journey home to again to someday be reunited with Tami and our higher deity.

— 31 —

Not feeling well for a few months, I still pressed on with my life.

I had lived many years without Tami, and over time, the sting of her loss left such a void in my heart that I relegated my situation, knowing neither could be filled or healed.

I was forever reminded every day in the still of the early morning hours. My missing her never went away or relented. I longed to once again reach out and gently touch her while she slept. What hurt even more was that I could no longer remember the soft, sweet scent of her soft skin.

What I was grateful for still being part of my life was my dog and constant companion, Lilly Belle. Afraid of dying and leaving her alone too long, I always made sure she had plenty of food and water and made emergency provisions for her to be picked up and taken care of.

After going through my long-accepted nighttime routine of tossing and turning, I finally fell asleep.

Waking up, I suddenly felt different.

Confused, I lifted my head above the pillow. Lilly Bell awoke with her ears softly tilted back. She gave me a sad, never-before-seen look of pure love, which confused and worried me.

Rising up, suddenly startled, I caught a glimpse of my body lying behind me as if I was still sleeping.

Realizing what was happening from Lilly Bell's reaction, uttering no words, I thought, *Thank you, God, for my life.*

Rising up with my eyes and spiritual mind, I conveyed to Lilly Belle, *Thank you, Lilly Belle, for watching and loving me all these years. If heaven is where I am bound, when you are ready, I hope God will allow dogs in heaven.* Smiling, I knew Lilly Belle could now understand me as I conveyed my last thoughts: *You won't be alone for long.* Feeling such love, I could not cry as my last Earthly thought was *I love you, Lilly.*

Fearing your mortality is only a concern for the living. The moment you die and only for a moment, you are now a spirit, and your real journey begins.

Rising up, I was not scared.

As I was going through a dark portal, my mind felt as if it was cleansing the past and becoming free of life's unnecessary blessings and burdens.

Appearing before me was a vision of beauty I had never seen before. The cotton-candy clouds, glowing white, were deeper and softer than I had ever seen. The sky, alive with colorful birds, once hunters and the hunted, peacefully flew together among the clouds. In stark contrast, the rich deep-blue sky was accentuated in depth and color. All were created for the enjoyment of the heavenly spirits.

Earthly, manmade sounds were gone. Only heaven, could be heard.

The flowers, vibrant and alive with color and sweet fragrances, filled my spirit as I walked along the lush deep-green grass pathway.

The mountains were blanketed with trees of all kinds and laced with waterfalls and streams of all sizes as God's white noise brought spiritual peace and beauty to His massive creation and sanctuary.

Taking this all in, I realized Earth was just a taste as God had saved the best of His creations for his spirits in heaven.

As I came to the end of the pathway, laid out before me was a huddled mass of bright, glowing white-bodied spirits. Approaching them in awe and wonderment, I suddenly realized they were my friends and relatives.

Standing in front, beaming, was my dad and mom with Imara and Bob.

I was happy to see them. Their years of earthly aging had been turned back; they now looked so young. I remembered long-ago ear-ly-aged earthly pictures of them. It seemed the heavenly clock of time had kindly been turned back. As heavenly spirits, their youth was restored. Unhindered by a body, they were in their prime now and forever.

I conveyed to all in thought, *What a wonderful thing to see all of you again.*

My mom smiled. *You have hair again!*

I reached up to check, and a bright smile washed over my face as I ran my fingers through my long-forgotten long hair.

It suddenly dawned on me. *Where's Tami?*

Imara slowly stepped forward. *Gary, she's not here.*

My heavenly aura dimmed. *This can't be.*

Falling on my knees, I covered my eyes with my hands as my spirit tried to cry but couldn't. Shaking my head in disbelief, I humbly whimpered, *Imara, a mistake has been made. This can't be. If Tami is in hell, then that is where I need to go. That is where I want to be, with her.* Raising my head, I prayed, *God, during my time on Earth, when I was living without her, heaven was where I pinned my hopes on Your grace and forgiveness so that we would be together again.*

Imara, in measured thought, said, *Gary, let me explain.*

Mom, there is no need for you to explain... I served my time on Earth. If spending my eternity here without Tami, and if this is going to be the outcome, then Heaven for me, is hell. So I might as well be with her. I forgave her for everything.

Pausing my thoughts, I slowly took my hands from my eyes. I noticed the parting of friends and relatives. I was confused. Both sets of my parents came close to me while putting their hands on my shoulders to share their love with me.

Suddenly my aura returned as my spiritual eyes filled with love at seeing Tami and Dirk standing before me. My thoughts overflowed with joy and happiness, blessing my spirit with peace.

With love-filled eyes, I conveyed, *It has been a long earthly time since you left. It is so nice to be with you.*

Dirk smiled. *It has been nice. Thank you for being a good husband to Tami.*

I smiled. *Dirk, we both were the lucky ones in having her as our wife. We both know she was worth it with the love that she gave back to both of us.* I stepped forward and embraced Tami. *Your mom scared* me. *I am so happy to be with you again. I guess you came up with the idea to tease me?*

Tami smiled. *Thanks! I thought of it, and just like down on Earth, I am still allowed to joke around… But just only a little bit!* Tami continued, *I have a surprise for you!* After turning her back to one of my friends, he gave her an object. Then she turned back and knelt down. *I thought you would like to have an old friend of ours join us!*

I was surprised and smiling. *Lilly Belle! Dogs* do *get to go to heaven!*

Tami passing her into my arms.

I paused for a moment, confused. *Tami…I just left her.*

She giggled. *Earth has a different time from heavenly time! I bet you didn't know I checked up on you and Lilly Belle quite often.*

I smiled as I hugged Lilly Belle. *Lilly Bell gave you away a few times! From time to time, I would see her give a loving look as she focused on something that I could not see. But I knew it was you.*

Tami continued, *Here, time is a funny thing that has its own schedule. Time is time, and regarding time as we knew it when we were alive, we were under its constraints. In heaven, time is just a portal to see, go, and do many things. The only thing that matters here is love. There is no longer any earthly need for hope because we don't need it. We already have everything we had ever hoped for or could hope for here. Time is no longer a factor as there is no time limit on eternity, and there is no longer any need to fear death as you have already done that!*

I was very happy and grateful, and my thought conveyed, *Being here and being with you here* is *heaven.*

Tami grinned. *Gary, you silly… This is Iowa! There is so much more to show you, and you ain't seen nothing yet!* Tami had a gleam of excitement in her eyes. *This is just the greeting area! Beyond the mountains awaits heaven and eternity!*